AMERICAN ESSA

SERIES EDITOR, EDWARD FOLEY

LITURGY AND HERMENEUTICS

Joyce Ann Zimmerman, C.PP.S.

A Liturgical Press Book

THE LITURGICAL PRESS
Collegeville, Minnesota

1   2   3   4   5   6   7   8   9

Library of Congress Cataloging-in-Publication Data

Zimmerman, Joyce Ann, 1945–
    Liturgy and hermeneutics / Joyce Ann Zimmerman.
      p. cm. — (American essays in liturgy)
    Includes bibliographical references and index.
    ISBN 0-8146-2497-9 (alk. paper)
    1. Catholic Church—Liturgy. 2. Hermeneutics—Religious aspects—Catholic Church. I. Title. II. Series: American essays in liturgy (Collegeville, Minn.)
    BX1970.5.Z55   1999
    264'.02'001—dc21
                              98-52226
                                 CIP

Contents

Introduction

Hermes is best known as his father Zeus' messenger, and it is his name that is the root for the word *hermeneutics,* the art of interpretation. But there is so much more to the ancient god Hermes than heralding messages. He is also a thief and trickster and patron of bargainers; he is the guide of souls to the underworld; in Homer's *Odyssey* he is portrayed as the wayfinder for travelers. All these images suggest to us that the art of interpretation is a tricky, multifaceted journey.

Moreover, Hermes' name has a root: *herm,* which was a square, stone post. Even before the gods, the ancient Greeks worshiped imageless stones to which they gave the name of gods. Eventually the stones were surmounted with heads and, finally, full bodies. In Hermes' origin and in his tasks we find engaging contrasts: "Hermes is a square post, Hermes is a winged messenger. No contrast it would seem could be more complete, no functions more incompatible. The whole gist of the Herm is to remain steadfast, the characteristic of the messenger is swift motion."[1] We return to this notion of contrast (we later call it a "dialectic") in subsequent chapters.

Hermeneutics—the art or science or theory of interpretation—is as many-faceted as the god from whom it derives its name. This is so because language itself is many-faceted. In some cases it would seem as though a clear denotation is evident. For example, if I were to say, "Liturgy begins at 10:00 A.M.," the message would seem to be clear. Yet, we could raise some questions: Does "liturgy" mean Mass? Morning Prayer? Devotional prayer? Does "10:00 A.M." mean

---

1. Jane Ellen Harrison, *Mythology* (New York and Burlingame: Harcourt, Brace & World, Inc., A Harbinger Book, 1963 [1924]) 6.

right on the dot at ten o'clock, or does it mean when everyone is gathered and ready?

In other cases a linguistic statement might clearly be connotative. For example, if I were to say, "The consecrated bread is truly the Body of Christ," I would presuppose or invite interpretation. The statement might raise questions about bread as a symbol, about the existential meaning of "is," about the force of truth, or about the modes of presence of the Body of Christ. In order to address such questions, the hearer would have to bring to bear on the statement such varied influences as her or his ritual understanding, Christian tradition, or symbolic theory.

All communication requires at least some interpretation, even if it is so minimal that the interlocutors are hardly aware of their interpretive activity. Most everyday conversation would fit this description. But a great deal of our communication is far more complex. Anytime we try to describe an idea or concept, a dream or religious experience, or try to relate to others our experience of art or music, we are well beyond ordinary language use and into the realm of language as symbol system. Since symbols have both a literal, at-hand meaning and another level of meaning available only through interpretation, much of our communication is hermeneutical.

Liturgy is certainly no exception to this generalization. Some members of Christian communities may pine for the days when it seemed as though everything about liturgy was clear and understandable and the rituals were denotative. However, we could make a strong case that the lack of interpretation of that perceived golden era deprived worshipers of the richness proper to liturgy. A non-interpretive approach to liturgy tends to reduce it to rubrics or received graces. We must likewise be wary of a too subjective interpretation of liturgy whereby the hermeneut shapes liturgy to her or his perception or need. Authentic interpretation plumbs liturgy's multivalent richness at the same time that it remains faithful to its tradition, doctrinal content, and ritual expression. This contrast, however, is no easy line to straddle.

The chapters of this book specifically address hermeneutics and its use in liturgy and liturgical studies. It might be well now, however, to briefly address the question "What is liturgy?" since the response to this question, too, is a hermeneutical exercise.

First and foremost, according to our Catholic tradition, liturgy makes present the mystery of Christ's dying and rising—so much so that the mystagogues, those early homilists who explained the initiation sacraments and their implication for Christian living to those who were newly baptized, simply referred to receiving baptism and Eucharist as receiving the "mysteries." Hear Cyril of Jerusalem: "This teaching of the blessed Paul [1 Cor 11:23f.] is in itself sufficient to assure you fully on the divine mysteries, through being accounted worthy of which you are now 'of the same body' and blood of Christ."[2] And from Theodore of Mopsuestia: "Christ our Lord established these awesome mysteries for us. . . . Accordingly at the sight of the bishop we form in our hearts a kind of image of Christ our Lord sacrificing himself to save us and give us life."[3]

Even more broadly, since Christian living also is about dying and rising—the paschal mystery in our everyday lives—we might further say that all of life is liturgy. A more restricted, official designation for liturgy is the celebration of all the sacraments and of the Liturgy of the Hours. For our purpose here, we generally refer to liturgy in terms of its official meaning. Further, since Eucharist is the most familiar liturgy to most of us, our examples are drawn largely from it.

Hermeneutics by its very nature is interdisciplinary, equally important for scholars of literature, philosophy, biblical texts, and theology. Nonetheless, this modest volume only speaks to the development and issues of hermeneutics as they are useful for the celebration and understanding of liturgy. Good introductions to general hermeneutics are available, and it may be useful to the reader to consult some of these.[4]

Nor do we speak to *theological methods* as such.[5] Our more restricted purpose is twofold: (1) to introduce the reader to a complex body of literature so that she or he can feel at least somewhat literate in a technical field without the need to master everything; and

2. IV:1 in Edward Yarnold, *The Awe-inspiring Rites of Initiation: The Origins of the R.C.I.A.*, 2nd ed. (Collegeville, Minn.: The Liturgical Press, 1994) 86.

3. IV:24 in Yarnold, *The Awe-inspiring Rites of Initiation*, 215.

4. See note 1, chapter 2.

5. The published material of writers who address questions of method—among them Gadamer, Pannenberg, Lonergan, Tracy—is vast. An example of one work by each on method includes Hans-Georg Gadamer, *Truth and Method*, trans. and rev. Joel Weinsheimer and Donald G. Marshall, 2nd rev. ed. (New York: Continuum, 1997); Wolfhart Pannenberg, *Anthropology in Theological Perspective*, trans. Matthew J. O'Connell (Philadelphia: The Westminster Press, 1985); Bernard Lonergan, *Method in Theology* (Toronto: University of Toronto Press, 1971); David Tracy, *Blessed Rage for Order: The New Pluralism in Theology* (New York: Seabury Press, 1975).

(2) to guide the reader through the complex issues and strategies involved in interpreting liturgy (as text, as ritual, as life). Our intent is not to promote a single hermeneutical approach as the "right one" but, instead, to point out advantages and disadvantages for a number of hermeneutical approaches.

To this end, Chapter 1 lays out the key issues and questions that a hermeneutical inquiry into liturgy necessarily raises. It delves into the involved issues that show us what is at stake when interpreting liturgy. Chapter 2 outlines a historical overview of the development of general hermeneutics. The guiding thread for this chapter is not a presentation of general hermeneutics, as such, but the shifts in its development that help us understand some of the liturgical interpretive issues challenging us today.

As a disciplinary branch of systematic theology, liturgical studies is in its infancy. Prior to this century, much of what was written on liturgy tended to be concerned with rubrics. This was certainly the case for seminary studies. Early Christian writers offer us a splendid approach to liturgy, both in terms of content and method, but it was largely lost when liturgy became the domain of clerics. Not until the liturgical movement beginning in the mid-nineteenth century and flowering in the decades before the Council did serious study of a *theology* of liturgy and a broader pastoral perspective become a reality.[6]

With so little liturgical hermeneutical method to draw on, it was only natural for the pioneers of liturgical theology to draw upon the same methods as biblical theology—that other discipline eminently concerned with sacred texts. Chapter 3 gives an overview of the strengths and weaknesses of the critical methods used in scriptural exegesis in order to make clear what questions these methods address and what questions are outside their venue. This sets up Chapter 4, which gives an overview of post-critical methods pertinent to the interpretation of liturgy.

Chapter 5 introduces the reader to some contemporary liturgists who are guided by particular hermeneutical issues. Finally, the Epilogue raises some questions yet to be addressed comprehensively by liturgists.

---

6. The Fathers of the Second Vatican Council asked us to "return to the sources." By this clarion call they underscored an approach to liturgy taking in more than rubrics. Ultimately, their cry for greater liturgical participation validated the liturgical movement and challenged us to continue to develop liturgical and pastoral liturgical theology.

At first glance, we might think that paying attention to schools of interpretation and method would be a rather dreary and boring liturgical enterprise. After all, is not liturgy a *celebration* of the paschal mystery, of all Christian living? Would not a volume on contemporary liturgical *practice* be far more interesting, engaging, and helpful? Or is this book intended only for the scholar who has the time to pay attention to esoteric questions?

The answer to the first question is yes, and the answer to the next two questions is no. Yes, liturgy is a celebration, but what do we mean by this? Some may interpret it as rhythmic clapping during a particularly spirited hymn or releasing helium balloons during an Ascension Thursday service. It is only with sound hermeneutical tools that we can begin to understand what is appropriate (interpret "appropriate" as whatever it is that makes present the paschal mystery) for *liturgical* celebration. This task can hardly be left only to academic liturgists, since all the practical decisions about liturgy are really made by pastoral personnel.

The answer to the next two questions is no because *anyone* engaged in the implementation of liturgy is necessarily interpreting the ritual for his or her own pastoral situation. The more tools at hand and the better the process is understood, the better the liturgical celebration. Therefore, this book is written for *anyone* interested in acquiring more and better tools for implementing liturgy.

The very first question recorded in Sacred Scripture is one the serpent put to the woman: "Did God say, 'You shall not eat from any tree in the garden'?" (Gen 3:1). Had that woman interpreted accurately both God's command and the serpent's wile, who knows where we might be today? The second question in Genesis is asked by God of both the woman and man: "Where are you?" (Gen 3:9); three more of God's questions follow (Gen 3:9-13). None of Adam's and Eve's responses directly answer God's questions; yet their evasions tell us clearly that they interpreted appropriately a shift in their relationship to God.

Liturgy empowers us to walk with God "in the garden at the time of the evening breeze" (Gen 3:8), an image that conjures up intimacy, familiarity, habitualness. This is what is at stake for us, too, when we are faced with interpreting appropriately those Christian rituals that make present for us, today, the divine mystery of God's salvific acts in the Son Jesus Christ. If this book contributes to realizing more authentic responses to God, then God be praised!

1 What's at Stake?

Just as Hermes was a god with many tasks, so is the art of interpretation complex and multifaceted. With respect to liturgy, three questions loom: Who interprets? What is the object of the interpretation? How do we interpret? These questions guide us in this chapter as we consider what's at stake in interpreting liturgy.

Who Interprets Liturgy?

At issue in this question is the competent authority for overseeing the liturgy of the Church. This is not so simple a question as it seems. Where official Church legislation is at hand—including but not limited to *Sacrosanctum Concilium*, various pieces of legislation from Rome (e.g., apostolic constitutions, apostolic letters *motu proprio*, and decrees), and the *Code of Canon Law*—the authority would seem fairly clear; but even this is not always the case. As R. Kevin Seasoltz remarks: "Because of the current ambiguity [with respect to the legal import of various documents], some documents that are relatively unimportant in content are given as much weight as those that are in fact very important. It often takes a skilled canonist to determine the legal import of texts, but at times not even the canonist can be sure of their weight."[1] Of course, another real issue ensues when interpretation of even seemingly clear statements is required.

1. R. Kevin Seasoltz, *New Liturgy, New Laws* (Collegeville, Minn.: The Liturgical Press, 1980) 181. Chapter 13 (pp. 169–181), "Canonical Significance of Conciliar, Papal, and Curial Pronouncements," is a helpful summary of different kinds of Roman documents and their juridical import.

Even a casual observer, however, knows full well that Roman documents do not begin to cover all the interpretations for possible choices when implementing a liturgical text. In fact, in addition to Roman documents, liturgical pronouncements—some with the import of particular law—are made by other competent authorities, for example, the International Commission on English in the Liturgy (ICEL, for English-speaking episcopal conference members), episcopal conferences, (arch)bishops in their own (arch)dioceses, pastors in their parishes, and parish liturgy commissions and directors—all to the extent that authority has been duly delegated to them.

Perhaps the most nettlesome authority is that resting with the liturgical assembly itself and the interpretation of a liturgy actually undertaken by individual members. Ultimately what is at stake in the authority of who interprets liturgy is not whether a particular rite is performed in a juridically correct or aesthetically pleasing manner, important as these aspects are, but whether members of the celebrating assembly appropriate for themselves the liturgical action, that is, whether the liturgy makes present the paschal mystery not only in the celebration of the ritual but in the everyday living of Christians. The goal of liturgy, then, is not so much perfect ritual as it is *prayer* that leads to appropriation of the Jesus-event in our lives. If a liturgy is performed flawlessly and according to liturgical law but does not make a difference in the lives of the people, then the liturgy ultimately has no authority, since it brings no life.

These remarks cannot be misconstrued: we are not subsuming competent liturgical authority under the pragmatic fruitfulness of liturgy in the lives of those who celebrate, much less under the whims of those who may choose what they like for appropriation and discard what they do not like. If this were the scenario, anyone would authentically interpret liturgy, and then liturgy itself would be robbed of any authoritative or prophetic import. The practical import of this is enormous. Many decisions concerning the implementation of a rite are not addressed in the official legislations, instructions, or interpretations. Seasoltz refers to the canonical axiom *de minimis non curat praetor.* This, he explains, "means that sometimes matters are of such minimal significance that it is not appropriate to make them the object of a canonical norm."[2] He offers as

2. Seasoltz, *New Liturgy, New Laws*, 207. All of his chapter 15 (pp. 202–211), "Fidelity to Law and Fidelity to Pastoral Needs," is pertinent to my point here.

one example the incorporation of liturgical movement (dance) in a rite. No law expressly permits such additions, yet we determine that it is not illicit to do so.

But other hermeneutical questions impinge upon our decision: Is the action appropriate for this time and place and for this liturgy? Is it pastorally sensitive? Has sufficient catechesis been offered so that the action will be understood, at least by the majority? Does the action enhance or disrupt the flow of the rite? Does the action enhance or disrupt the assembly's prayer? Does the action help draw the assembly more deeply into the paschal mystery? If we consider seriously these kinds of questions, it becomes apparent that nothing we do in deviation from the general norm is so minor that we ought not give it serious attention.

Sometimes the law itself is contradictory, ambiguous, or gives options that must be interpreted. For example, the General Instruction of the Roman Missal leaves open options for which liturgical actions take place at the ambo, stating that the responsorial psalm at a Eucharistic celebration takes place "at the lectern or other suitable place" (no. 36). Number 272 implies that a broad range of functions may take place at the ambo: proclamation (of the readings and Easter *Exsultet*), response (psalm), acclamation (for the gospel), homily, and announcement of intentions at the general intercessions. It then goes on to say that it "is better for the commentator, cantor, or choir director not to use the lectern."[3]

Obviously, some interpretation is needed, and this is a practical issue facing every liturgical community. If the sanctuary space is very small, there may be no choice but to use the ambo for everything permitted. However, if space is sufficient, then someone must decide what is to happen where. If we reserve the ambo only for one function, proclamation—a determination that may derive from thinking through (interpreting) a theology of the Liturgy of the Word—then at least the responsorial psalm, gospel acclamation, and announcement of the intentions would take place elsewhere.[4]

---

3. ICEL, *Documents on the Liturgy 1963–1979: Conciliar, Papal, and Curial Texts* (Collegeville, Minn.: The Liturgical Press, 1982) 520. All quotations from the General Instruction of the Roman Missal are taken from this volume.

4. Elsewhere I have argued that the homily is proclamation, so it would fittingly take place at the ambo (see my "Homily as Proclamation," *Liturgical Ministry* 1 [1992] 10–16), although the General Instruction (no. 97) implies that the preferred place is from the chair, since that is the first choice given.

Just as we saw Hermes as the god who embodies contrasts between steadfastness and swift motion, so is the competent authority of liturgy a matter of contrasts (or creative tension or dialectic). The legislation, instructions, and official interpretations of liturgy must remain in dialectical relationship with what is pastorally effective and appropriate for a given liturgy in a given liturgical assembly. Recognized competent authority must remain in dialectical relationship with the celebrating liturgical assembly. This is not always an easy balance to maintain. Generally, the more critical the questions, the more difficult is it to make decisions.[5] Absolutely essential to decisions concerning critical questions is a clearly articulated liturgical theology from which the community operates. Without such a theological framework, decisions can be inconsistent at best and misleading at worst.

At stake in the question "Who interprets liturgy?" is the realization that the practice of liturgy involves a number of competencies at a number of levels.[6] All must be respected. In the case of clear conflict, the weight of the legislation must be balanced with pastoral sensitivity. This may not always leave everyone satisfied, but it does ensure that liturgy remains faithful to its tradition at the same time that it respects pastoral sensitivity.

What Is Interpreted?

The object of liturgical interpretation is also not quite so apparent as our second question might suggest. The most simple answer

5. I would direct the reader to John Huels' two volumes (*Disputed Questions in the Liturgy Today* and *More Disputed Question in the Liturgy,* both from Liturgical Training Publications, Chicago) for a fine example of someone who tackles difficult pastoral liturgy questions and balances legislation and pastoral practice.

6. Critical here is the issue of liturgical formation. All too often the very ones who actually make liturgical decisions are the ones least formed in liturgical theology and least exposed to the directives of competent authority. Those parish personnel who make liturgical decisions cannot be expected to be up on every piece of liturgical legislation that comes along. Nor can they be expected to be liturgical theologians. Nevertheless, these people must know (or find out) at least the basics of doing good liturgy. They ought to be familiar with the Constitution on the Sacred Liturgy, the general instructions accompanying the revised rites, and have some familiarity with a liturgical theology and the ability to articulate it.

is "the liturgical text," but that response demands a great deal of nuance and interpretation.

Liturgical texts may be divided into two general categories: primary and secondary texts. Primary texts are those that are directly concerned with the celebration of liturgy itself; these would generally include the ritual books, the actual enactment of the ritual, and Christian living insofar as its dynamic parallels the structural dynamic of liturgy.[7] Secondary texts would include all the legislation, instructions, explanations, and interpretations of those primary texts. Before we can address these texts as objects of interpretation, it is imperative that we briefly consider text theory. Exactly what is meant by "text"?

A Viable Text Theory for Liturgy

It would take us too far afield to survey comprehensively text theory in this essay or even to lay out the main lines of its development. More important for our purpose is to outline a text theory that seems comprehensive enough to encompass a broad notion of liturgical text. For this we turn to the French philosopher Paul Ricoeur.[8]

---

7. See my *Liturgy as Living Faith: A Liturgical Spirituality* (Scranton, Pa.: University of Scranton Press/London and Toronto: Associated University Presses, 1993) *passim*, but especially pp. 133–136. In that volume I argue that both liturgy and Christian living have the same structural dynamic and a common referent, the paschal mystery.

8. One of the difficulties with working in Ricoeur is that he is a prolific writer who tends not to publish systematic tomes on a given subject. The closest thing to an available volume on text theory is the publication of four lectures given in 1973 at Texas Christian University: *Interpretation Theory: Discourse and the Surplus of Meaning* (Fort Worth, Tex.: The Texas Christian University Press, 1976). The four lectures (chapters in the volume) are titled "Language as Discourse," "Speaking and Writing," "Metaphor and Symbol," and "Explanation and Understanding." For a summary of the breadth of his writings delving into "What is a text?" see my *Liturgy as Language of Faith: A Liturgical Methodology in the Mode of Paul Ricoeur's Textual Hermeneutics* (Lanham, New York, London: University Press of America, 1988) 61–69, 71–103.

I do not mean to imply that Ricoeur's is the only approach to liturgical text we might take. Since this volume is an introduction to liturgical hermeneutics, a comprehensive text *theory* is essential. Other liturgists have productively taken other approaches to texts, but not specifically within the parameters of a theory of liturgical hermeneutics. For two other approaches to text, see Lawrence A. Hoffman, *Beyond the Text: A Holistic Approach to Liturgy* (Bloomington and Indianapolis, Ind.: Indiana University Press, 1987) and Kevin W.

15

For most of us, "text" conjures up the massive amount of printed material we somehow manage to devour on a regular basis. For the hermeneutical process, however, text is a paradigm of interpretation with a much broader domain of potential data (meaning) than just written texts. Ricoeur takes text to mean any *document* of life[9] composed by preaccepted rules[10] in a particular style. Thus, a sand configuration formed by blowing wind would not be a text, but a sandcastle built by a small (and sometimes not so small) child would be a text. Within the parameters of this broad notion of text, a painting, sculpture, music, choreographed dance would all be texts. What, then, is really at stake when we refer to something as a text?

Long before Gutenberg and the information explosion, Western cultures were oral. Communication was largely limited to an event between two or more persons present to each other. The import of personal proximity is that misunderstandings can be checked immediately by the interlocutors, clarifying vocabulary and ideas between or among themselves. In some respects this is an ideal form of communication because, presumably, misunderstandings can be kept to an absolute minimum. However, oral communication is fleeting; once the event is over (when the interlocutors part company), the meaning of the exchange might remain in the memory of the interlocutors but is unavailable for anyone else.

Ancient cultures were clearly not interested in limiting their communication to fleeting discourse. We have evidence first of pictures, then of symbolic markings, and then of alphabets that enabled the fleeting character of discourse to be shifted to fixed marks on cave walls, stone, papyrus, and paper that convey a message.

Irwin, *Context and Text: Method in Liturgical Theology* (Collegeville, Minn.: The Liturgical Press, 1994); both of these authors are discussed in Chapter 5.

9. Cf. Paul Ricoeur, "The Model of the Text: Meaningful Action Considered as a Text" in *Hermeneutics and the Human Sciences: Essays on Language, Action and Interpretation,* ed. and trans. John B. Thompson (Cambridge: Cambridge University Press, 1981) 206.

10. In the case of written texts, these rules are what we refer to as a "literary genre." Even other kinds of texts follow genre rules. For example, liturgy is a particular genre of ritual which, in turn, is a particular genre of human action. Something that intrigues me and points to an important area for further liturgical research is determining and describing adequately what is a "liturgical genre," that is, what is the unique genre that gives the rules for composing *liturgical* texts (see my *Liturgy as Language of Faith,* 69, 166–170).

This tremendous cultural achievement equipped people to communicate meaning *beyond* the instance of an event by fixing meaning for recovery at a later time.[11] A relationship as well as a significant difference ensues between event and meaning. Meaning is that which is fixed in a text; meaning is the residue of event that can be recovered. Meaning is repeatable.[12]

These remarks suggest that a text witnesses to human living while at the same time enjoying an autonomy of its own. To interpret a text is at the same time to interpret human living *without* returning to the actual interlocutors and situation(s) that produced the text.[13] A text endures in time, and therefore it enjoys a certain autonomy, something that is not true for fleeting human discourse. A text embodies a residue of meaning originating in the discourse but surpassing it. The task of hermeneutics is to uncover this residue of meaning.

Ricoeur takes this dialectic of event and meaning a step further when he asserts that human action (for example, gestures, movements, postures) can also be fixed in a text.[14] Ritual is a good example of the fixation of human action. Rituals are rule-governed; they are executed according to a written or unwritten set of rules. This is the fixed meaning enabling the ritual to be repeated—so the encoded meaning is recoverable. With respect to liturgical texts, the residue of meaning recoverable by its fixation remains constant throughout liturgical tradition, even though the specific ceremonial that concretely shapes it changes from time to time. One can distinguish, therefore, between "prescriptive" and "normative" in this regard,[15] with prescriptive having to do with the ceremony and style, and normative having to do with the tradition. To interpret a liturgical text is to interpret a liturgical tradition.

11. See Ricoeur, *Interpretation Theory*, 25–29.

12. See Zimmerman, *Liturgy as Language of Faith*, 48–49.

13. As we see in Chapters 3 and 4, the exact relationship of interpretation to a text's author (or the event that gave rise to a text) is a key distinction between critical and post-critical methods.

14. See his essay "The Model of the Text: Meaningful Action Considered as a Text" in *Hermeneutics and the Human Sciences*, 197–221. For a summary of Ricoeur's action theory, see my *Liturgy as Living Faith*, 44–51.

15. See my *Liturgy as Language of Faith*, 129, esp. n. 4. We also refer to "surface structure" (what is at hand, i.e., the text or ritual) and "deep structure" (what is the meaning). See below, p. 65, for the importance of these concepts in the development of hermeneutics.

Let's pause to clarify further the notion of meaning. For Ricoeur, meaning is the dialectic of sense and reference. Sense is the "what is said" and reference is the "about what." Reference is uncovered in the depth-meaning of language in use and points to extra-textual reality. Reference bears the ontological vehemence of a text as the "world" of discourse, the "about which" proper to a text. Text has both a *surface* structure, which is its at-hand organization (genre and style), and a *deep* structure, which is its recoverable trace of human activity (life).[16] Meaning is a dialectic between linguistic structure and life structure.

Further, in particular kinds of discourse (Ricoeur draws heavily on poetic discourse), there is a "split" sense and reference. That is, one level of sense (the literal) delivers up an obvious reference, and, additionally, a second, only implied sense opens up an innovative world of reference. The ontological question really opens up when we take this one step further: the process of interpretation involves an interaction between the world (reference) of the text and the world of the interpreter. Hermeneutics persists in reminding us that interpretation makes a difference in the interpreter. An example may help make this clear.

Let's consider communion bread. When we take and eat the bread, its literal sense says "bread" (hopefully, it looks and tastes like bread, which is not always the case and poses another problem for interpretation); the reference that this literal sense opens up for us is bread as the staff of life that nourishes and sustains. In the context of Eucharist, the literal sense of bread implies another world: the Body of Christ, which is our participation in the messianic banquet and spiritually nourishes and sustains us in our identity as Christians. The sense of bread is "split," so that the literal sense and reference open up for us another, deeper sense and reference.

Liturgy as Text, Ritual, Life

The contrast of event and meaning (Ricoeur refers to this as a dialectic) can help us clarify the previously mentioned problematic

16. For example, the Eucharistic liturgy's surface structure would include the invariable order of the introductory rites, Liturgy of the Word, Liturgy of the Eucharist, and concluding rite. It would also include such elements as style of music, use of silences, and rhythm of celebrations during the various liturgical seasons. The Eucharistic liturgy's deep structure would be the dying and rising of the paschal mystery that it makes present.

with respect to the liturgical text as text, ritual, or life. Ritual is always an *event*. As such, it is fleeting; it happens in time and then is over. No two rituals are alike, because each worshiping community celebrates the ritual in a particular time and space and at a particular instance in their lives. The liturgical text, on the other hand, is fixed in writing.[17] It is repeatable and shapes the specific ritual of a liturgical community. Innumerable individual rituals enact a given liturgical text. Without the liturgical text, the meaning of the liturgical ritual could not be shared among all worshiping communities and passed on in the tradition. Indeed, there could not even be liturgical tradition.

Liturgical interpretation encompasses two initial objects: the ritual and the text, the event and the fixed meaning. Since we are dealing with dialectics, the meaning of the event and the fixed meaning are not identical; there is always a residue of meaning in interpretation. For this reason, limiting the hermeneutical task of the liturgist to either the ritual or the text is to limit the richness of meaning that can be recovered.[18] Different methods may be used to interpret rituals from those used to interpret the texts.[19]

Another object of liturgical interpretation is Christian living itself, since liturgy and Christian living are both about making present the paschal mystery. Problematic, though, is the fact that Christian living is particular, involves a great number of people, and extends over a long period of time. Any direct interpretation of Christian living would necessarily be tentative and limited. This does not preclude the value of interpreting Christian living; it just restricts the theoretical generalizations that might be drawn. Christian spirituality has a long tradition of interpreting living; its basic

17. Obviously, my remarks here are pertinent only for those liturgical communities that celebrate a fixed text. Interestingly enough, though, many communities without a fixed worship text evolve a ritual pattern that in practice serves as a fixed (though not binding) text.

18. A similar dialectic poses itself for Scripture scholars: Is the Word of God in the text or in its proclamation?

19. Ronald Grimes is one current researcher who has done extensive field studies in ritual and constructed ritual theory based on those field studies. See his "Emerging Ritual" in *Proceedings of the North American Academy of Liturgy,* Annual Meeting at Saint Louis, January 2–5, 1990 (Valparaiso, Ind.: North American Academy of Liturgy, 1990) 15–31. See also his *Beginnings in Ritual Studies* (Washington: University Press of America, 1982). I have been one who has focused interpretation on the text itself. See my *Liturgy as Language of Faith.*

tool is an examination of conscience (in whatever its form). Lent is a liturgical season given us to interpret our Christian living. Although these exercises may be helpful, the most direct interpretation of Christian living is by means of interpreting either the liturgical ritual or the text. Thus, these are the primary objects to which liturgical interpretation is directed.

How Are Texts Interpreted?

One final question to address in assessing what is at stake in liturgy and hermeneutics is a methodological one. The "how" question takes us to method.

Above we defined meaning as a dialectic of sense and reference. This is the key dialectic in the textual moment—key because reference pushes us beyond the text. Sense is immanent in a text; reference points beyond the text. Another dialectic important for Ricoeur's textual hermeneutics is that between explanation and understanding. This is the dialectic key to the methodic moment—key because, for Ricoeur, understanding has an ontological vehemence. In Ricoeur's hermeneutic method, explanation is an analytic exercise that is directed toward the *sense* of the text. It is *through* explanation that the deep structure, the integrating dynamic of a text, is delivered up as the world (reference) of the text available to the hermeneut as new possibilities for human action. Ricoeur's methodic hermeneutics requires both an analytic moment and a new moment of self-understanding.

This essay on liturgy and hermeneutics primarily addresses the analytic moment. In Chapter 2 we outline different *theories* of interpretation by developing the field of general hermeneutics. In Chapters 3 and 4 we address some specific methods for interpreting liturgical texts. Anyone interpreting texts must keep in mind that a method is necessarily limited; this one looks at this piece of the text, that one at another piece. No one method can uncover the full or deepest meaning of a text. A hermeneut chooses a method because it promises to deliver an answer to a particular set of questions. This necessarily implies that the interpreter must let go of other questions, or address them in another interpretive moment (by using another method). No one interpretive method can deliver the whole meaning of a text; meaning and interpretation are dynamic. This further suggests that when differing interpretations (interpreters) are in dialogue, a fuller meaning is released.

Response to the Question

What is at stake in interpreting liturgy? Certainly, the authority of the interpreter, the text being interpreted, and the method employed are all critical concerns. If liturgy were simply an abstract entity, there could be much breadth and tolerance in each of these areas. Unlike most other texts, however, liturgical texts hold meaning that has living and salvific implications. Thus the interpretation of liturgical texts is hardly a moot or simply academic exercise. A deeper grasp of the liturgical text affords us a greater insight into the very meaning of our lives. This is what is at stake.

2 Overview of Hermeneutical Theory and Issues

The inquiry into hermeneutical theory that occupies us in this chapter is readily available in general introductory volumes on hermeneutical theory and its development. It is not my intent to repeat this work here nor even to summarize these volumes as such.[1] Instead, my intent is to continue the liturgical discussion begun in Chapter 1, but now with a specific focus on how the various issues of hermeneutical theory affect liturgy and its interpretation.

The chapter is divided into two main sections. The first gives a brief overview of the development of hermeneutics. This is designed to be helpful for the reader who has little background in general hermeneutics. The second section of the chapter deals more specifically with the issues of general hermeneutics and their import for liturgical studies.

1. See, for example, Jean Grondin, *Introduction to Philosophical Hermeneutics* (New Haven and London: Yale University Press, 1994); also his *Sources of Hermeneutics* (New York: State University of New York Press, 1995); Werner G. Jeanrond, *Theological Hermeneutics: Development and Significance* (New York: Crossroad, 1991); Richard E. Palmer, *Hermeneutics* (Evanston, Ill.: Northwestern University Press, 1969); David Klemm, ed., *Hermeneutical Inquiry*, 2 vols., American Academy of Religion Studies in Religion 43/44 (Atlanta: Scholars Press, 1986); Anthony C. Thiselton, *New Horizons in Hermeneutics: The Theory and Practice of Transforming Biblical Reading* (Grand Rapids, Mich.: Zondervan Publishing House, 1992); *The Hermeneutics Reader: Texts of the German Tradition from the Enlightenment to the Present*, ed. with intro. and notes by Kurt Mueller-Vollmer (New York: Continuum, 1985); Josef Bleicher, *Contemporary Hermeneutics: Hermeneutics as Method, Philosophy and Critique* (London, Boston and Henley: Routledge and Kegan Paul, 1980).

First, a clarification. Specialists in the field of hermeneutics distinguish between general and specific hermeneutics. General hermeneutics explores hermeneutical theory and is especially interdisciplinary, often requiring at least some expertise in philosophy, linguistics, philology, and literary criticism. Methodology figures little in general hermeneutics, except insofar as various methodologies are discussed as a way to illustrate the application of a particular theoretical stance. Specific hermeneutics applies to a particular field of study, for example, literature or theology or Sacred Scripture. Freud's dream interpretation could be considered a specific hermeneutic, as could the film reviews of Siskel and Ebert. Methodology (the subject of Chapters 3 and 4) plays a critical role in specific hermeneutics; in fact, they are so intertwined as to be barely distinguishable from one another. In this chapter we are concerned with general hermeneutics.

Overview of the Development of Hermeneutics

Ancient Greeks

The use of the term "hermeneutics" is rather late, first appearing in the sixteenth century. Its operations, nonetheless, go back as far as the ancient Greeks. We related in the Introduction how Hermes was the Greek's messenger god. It was his task to interpret for humans the will of the gods. Similarly, it was the poets' task in Greek society to interpret those messages of the gods. Thus, in its earliest stage, hermeneutics had to do with determining how to live in society. This interpreting-for-life became an important aspect of Greek society, especially with their great literary works (e.g., the works of Homer).

The Greeks had three meanings or uses for interpretation.[2] First, hermeneutics was used to express or to say something. Second, hermeneutics was used to explain (e.g., Homer's works). Third, hermeneutics was used "to translate." From these three ancient meanings evolved three separate fields of inquiry: discourse and communication theory (to express or say something), hermeneutics proper (to explain), and philology (to translate). Our contemporary meaning of hermeneutics may involve all three ancient uses,

---

2. Cf. ἑρμηνεύω in *Theological Dictionary of the New Testament*, ed. Gerhard Kittel, trans. and ed. Geoffrey W. Bromiley (Grand Rapids, Mich.: Wm. B. Eerdmans, 1964) 2:661–663.

but the second meaning more closely resembles hermeneutic activity today.

The Sophists developed the ancient art of interpretation to a high degree—actually, to an art. Called rhetoric, it was the art of "beautiful speech." Their concern was directed to clear, exquisitely constructed, *persuasive* speech. Any discourse that did not move the hearer to the particular viewpoint or proposed course of action of the speaker was considered not beautiful. Accordingly, speech was considered beautiful not only because the images and sonority were aesthetically pleasing but because the discourse persuaded the hearers to a viewpoint or course of conduct.

Let's take a familiar liturgical example: What makes a sermon or homily "beautiful"? Sometimes we hear eloquent preachers, but we sense that their homily lacks content, it is empty. It may be beautiful by certain standards of literary rules and poetic constructs, but it is not beautiful (according to the mores of Greek rhetoric) because it does not move the assembly. On the other hand, sometimes we hear sermons and homilies that touch us deeply and stir within us convictions to act charitably, justly, humbly, etc. These preachers would be considered rhetoricians by Greek standards, and the homily would be considered beautiful.[3]

The Greeks contributed two important viewpoints for an understanding of general hermeneutics; these are taken up as two opposing positions in modern hermeneutics and are critical for grasping the contemporary debates. We make a few brief remarks here, but more extensive comments are made in the next section of this chapter.

First, interpretation has to do with *life*. As we mentioned, the Greeks understood expressing and translating as interpretive activities, but their chief sympathies lay with interpretation as explaining—rhetoric—and that had to do directly with how one lives. In other words, interpretation always has a stake in how we live.

Second, the *art* of interpretation, that is, interpretation that persuades, is practiced by recognized "professionals." It is not an activity for the common person. In Greek society, the poets and rhetoricians had a particular standing within society because they were the ones who were skilled in explaining the codes of conduct for living. In other words, interpretive explaining had something to

---

3. See James M. Schmitmeyer, *The Words of Worship: Presiding and Preaching at the Rites* (New York: Alba House, 1988) 14–15, for one homilist who recognizes the value of rhetoric for Christian preaching.

do with what was valued in society. Ordinary folk might explain why the crops failed, but it was the poets, orators, and rhetoricians who explained life. The ordinary person in the pew might recognize the dying and rising in their everyday living, but it is the creative, insightful liturgist who explains the relationship between the dying and rising and liturgy.

Early Christian Interpretive Tradition

As might be expected, the earliest Christian hermeneutic has to do with explaining the Jesus event. We might rightfully say that Paul was probably the first great Christian hermeneut.[4] The Acts of the Apostles includes a number of (fragmented) homilies that could also be considered to be the beginnings of a Christian hermeneutical tradition. Indeed, the onset of Christian hermeneutics came in the form of homilies, not theological tracts. In fact, the entire patristic period is rich in a homiletic tradition that is solidly in the line of the rhetorical tradition.[5]

Irenaeus of Lyons (d. ca. 202) was an early writer concerned with adequate principles of interpretation. Faced with the false interpretations of the Gnostics, Irenaeus was perhaps the first to address (the modern problem of) the conflict of interpretations. His solution was to "complement his hermeneutical demand for adequate interpretation with an ecclesiastical criterion . . . [a] norm, represented solely by the apostolic tradition in the church, Irenaeus called 'the canon of truth' *(regula veritatis).*"[6]

Early in the patristic tradition, two main "schools" of interpretation emerged, the Alexandrian and Antiochene, both of which had Scripture as their object of interpretation. Origen (d. ca. 254) aligned himself with the Alexandrian school (allegorical interpretation) and was the first Christian hermeneut to offer a systematic theory of interpretation. He "distinguished a threefold structure of textual sense: lit-

4. Interpretation of salvific events is not unique to Christians. All the great religious traditions have written scriptures, each with its own history of interpretation. Since Paul was a trained Pharisee who belonged to the school of Gamaliel, it would be naive to say that he was cut off from a long and rich tradition of Hebrew Scripture interpretation. The body of rabbinic and midrashic literature alone attests to this great tradition.

5. For a very fine overview of the development of Christian preaching, see J. Kevin Coyle, "From Homily to Sermon to Homily: The Content of Christian Preaching in Historical Perspective," *Liturgical Ministry* 1 (1992) 3–9.

6. Jeanrond, *Theological Hermeneutics*, 20.

eral, moral and spiritual. In practice, however, he distinguished only between 'letter' and 'spirit.'"[7] Because the Scriptures dealt with the ultimate mystery of God's revelation to humankind, they necessarily used language veiled in symbols. Thus interpretation sought the higher levels of meaning. Moreover, the Christian canon cannot be separated from the Hebrew canon. Allegorical interpretation saw all kinds of figurative connections between the two canons. The waters of baptism are foreshadowed, for example, by the destructive waters of the Red Sea, by the flood, by the life-giving waters at Meribah, and by Naaman, the gentile leper who bathed in the river Jordan.

Tertullian (d. ca. 220) is an example of a proponent of the Antiochene school, which opted for a more literal approach to the scriptural text. Although they saw a correspondence between certain events of the Hebrew Scriptures and the Christ-event, they did not draw out the extended literary comparisons of details of events that was characteristic of the Alexandrian school of interpretation. A comparison may help to understand the difference between these two interpretive schools. Ambrose of Milan, who probably was persuaded to the allegorical method of interpretation by reading Origen, refers to the Jewish people passing through the Red Sea as a type for baptism. But does not stop there; he extends the comparison by mentioning that all the Jews who passed through the Red Sea died in the desert, but the one who passes through baptismal waters does not die but rises to new life.[8] Theodore of Mopsuestia, on the other hand, representing the Antiochene school of more literal interpretation, simply mentions that the water is a "crucible" in which the baptized is reshaped to a higher nature.[9]

Augustine (d. 430) "brought both of these hermeneutical traditions to a new synthesis."[10] He linked an allegorical art of interpretation with empirical exegesis and distinguished two kinds of scriptural passages requiring interpretation: "obscurities," that is, those passages whose meaning has been concealed by time, language, and different cultural customs; and "mysteries," that is, those passages concealing divine knowledge available only to scholars but not to the ignorant reader. Augustine accepted the

---

7. Ibid., 21.
8. *De sacramentis* I:12. In I:23 he mentions the flood as prefiguring baptism; in II:8 he mentions Naaman the leper.
9. Third baptismal homily, no. 11.
10. Jeanrond, *Theological Hermeneutics*, 22.

cultural priority of Latin as the language of theology, and so much of his interpretation is a semiotic approach. For Augustine, the text points to reality. This moves the question of interpretation beyond adequate interpretive theory to interpretation as a question of praxis. Augustine offered a unique reading perspective for the Christian hermeneut: love. By means of this reading perspective, he attempted a more systematic approach to a theory of interpretation.[11]

It may seem that these and other early Christian hermeneuts focused more on method than theory. Nonetheless, we can see here the same theoretical concern that the Greeks gave us: the relationship of interpretation and praxis.

From Medieval to Modern Hermeneutics

Medieval hermeneutics gradually separated the sacred text from its interpretation, introducing a distance between Scripture and theology. Gone was the era in which theology was essentially constructed through homilies, firmly grounded in interpretation of Scripture texts. Now theologians were preoccupied with a multiplicity of words and reality that had to be brought into some kind of unity. There was a need to find universals. The Reformation theologians attempted to return to *sola Scriptura,* and in so doing became interested in patristic interpretations. But they were limited by their own founding texts.

Modern Hermeneutics

Modern hermeneutics traces its beginnings to the middle of the eighteenth century and introduced an expanded domain for hermeneutics that included psychology, history, sociology, and anthropology. Modern hermeneutics, in fact, began with a struggle to place the methods of human sciences on a scientific par with the methods of the natural sciences. No more is hermeneutics limited to interpreting certain founding texts, but now all texts are within the province of hermeneutics.

It is impossible to trace all the thinkers and theories contributing to where we are today with respect to hermeneutics. For our pur-

11. It is interesting to note that Augustine's reading perspective of love is not limited to interpreting Scripture. In *De catechizandis rudibus*, Augustine proposes a question/answer dialogue for teaching the one to be catechized (brought to a fine art in the sentences of the Scholastics) and admonishes "yet, with how much love is one who is inferior fired when he discovers that he is loved by him who is superior" (4:7).

poses, we limit our discussion to six major figures: Schliermacher, Dilthey, Heidegger, Gadamer, Habermas, and Ricoeur. Further, our discussion focuses primarily on each thinker's approach to understanding. By limiting ourselves thus, we hope to make clearer the issues that bear directly on grasping the significance of hermeneutical development for liturgical studies.[12]

1. Friedrich Schliermacher (1768–1834). Schliermacher is generally accepted as the "father of modern hermeneutics." He gained this title because he was the first to move hermeneutics beyond exegesis of texts to a general theory of understanding. Understanding is an *art* and whenever it is achieved, it is guided by interpretation, which in turn is guided by explicit rules of language. Schliermacher represents an important shift from language to the subject, which is at the heart of hermeneutics even to the present day.

Schliermacher came into contact with German Romantics while a pastor and professor in Berlin, and for him understanding is reconstructing the thinking of another person.[13] Some scholars critique Schliermacher for a too psychological approach to interpretation, but his later writings contribute a linguistic corrective. For Schliermacher, then, interpretation is a process involving both language and the author's thought. Counteracting his Romanticist tendencies, he held that language has a grammar, that is, it is rule-produced. One aspect of the interpretive process grasps the sense in language with the help of language. Another aspect of the interpretive process is "divinatory," that technical or psychological process that focuses on meaning rather than on the truth of a text and seeks to grasp the whole or unity of a work in its composition.

In his two-part interpretive process, Schliermacher "emphasizes on the one hand that divination must not be understood as an individualistic escape from given semantic facts, and on the other hand that no (objective) knowledge of the text's linguistic composition can ever replace the interpreter's obligation to grasp the text's overall sense, although such a grasp will at best lead only to an approximate reconstruction" of the thinking of the author.[14] Because language follows defined rules and because texts are constructed according to

---

12. Each of these thinkers made a major theological and/or philosophical contribution beyond his hermeneutical contribution.

13. The Romanticists sought to understand a text as well as or even better than the author.

14. Jeanrond, *Theological Hermeneutics*, 47.

rules of composition, the sense of a text is accessible by paying attention to these rules. This rescues Schliermacher's hermeneutics from mere subjectivism. The counterpart to this more objective process of interpretation is the desire to recover the author's thought. This two-part interpretive process is consistent with Schliermacher's agenda to show how thought and linguistic expression are related.

Schliermacher's contribution to modern hermeneutics lies in his extending specific hermeneutics to a general, philosophical hermeneutics, a discipline in its own right rather than a subdiscipline of theology, jurisprudence, or literary criticism. As important as this development was, it remained largely untapped for a century. Then philosophical hermeneutics was taken up by Dilthey.

2. Wilhelm Dilthey (1833–1911). Dilthey entered the hermeneutical foray by writing a biography of Schliermacher. Dilthey had a lifelong interest in biography and is considered the founder of "life philosophy." "Life" is all of reality about which we can think and can only be understood in terms of its expressions (mediations). These life expressions include concepts, judgments, and ideas or human action or expressions of lived experience. It follows, then, that Dilthey's is an imposing hermeneutic largely concerned with authorial psychology. Understanding, for him, is intention or mental content.

Dilthey brought hermeneutics into contact with nineteenth century philosophy. If Kant showed how natural science is possible and uses exact methods based on demonstration, Dilthey wished to demonstrate the validity of the human sciences and made the distinction between methodologies appropriate for the natural sciences and those for the human sciences. The natural sciences *explain* natural phenomenon; the human sciences *understand* human life.[15] Science can deal with a phenomenon abstractly in a laboratory; the laboratory of the human sciences is life itself, which can only be interpreted through its mediations in a particular context. The works of the *historical* human being are the objects of interpretation. Hermeneutics deals with meanings intelligible in a context rather than with the abstract facts that are the domain of the physical sciences.

Dilthey, too, is faulted for a too psychological approach to hermeneutics. He stands in a direct line with the hermeneutical tradition concerned with interpreting written texts; as such, he is also

15. Here we can see the beginnings of a critical distinction in hermeneutics between explanation and understanding—between epistemology and ontology—taken up by later hermeneuts.

concerned with author and authorial intention. According to Dilthey, the highest form of understanding comes when the hermeneut (the reader of the written text) achieves total empathy with the author. The ideal is that the reader *relive* the emotions, feelings, and circumstances that were first experienced by the author and were then conveyed to a written text. The reader reverses the process: first, undertaking historical research to enter into the context or world of the author; second, "reading" the written expression to, third, enter into the author's original experience. Understanding, then, is grasping the mind of the author.

Dilthey's hermeneutics, however, is a step beyond the Romanticist tendencies of Schliermacher. The difference is that Dilthey focused on *interpretation* of the traces of human life on phenomena rather than on *introspection* (a psychological approach).[16] As Dilthey gradually came to sever interpretation from the author and focus on interpretation of the objectifications of life in historical context, he was able to "envision the possibility of objectively valid knowledge, since the object was relatively unchanging in itself."[17] Further, because traces of human life on phenomena call for "historical rather than scientific modes of understanding," Dilthey upheld that the object of interpretation "could only be understood through reference to life itself in all its historicality and temporality."[18] Although Dilthey never quite extricated himself from searching for a methodological objectivity for the human sciences that paralleled that of the natural sciences, he did advance the hermeneutical project in an important direction: historicality. The question of time and being occupied Heidegger, as we see next.

3. Martin Heidegger (1889–1976). Heidegger was first and foremost a phenomenological philosopher and was not primarily concerned with philosophical hermeneutics. Nonetheless, he was key in moving hermeneutics into fundamental ontology and triggered the definitive shift from psychologism to being-in-the-world.

Sein und Zeit is Heidegger's great work.[19] He clearly sets out his aim: "to work out the question of the meaning of *Being* and to do so concretely. Our provisional aim is the Interpretation of *time* as the

---

16. See Palmer, *Hermeneutics,* 104 and 121.

17. Ibid., 121.

18. Ibid., 122.

19. English edition: *Being and Time,* trans. John Macquarrie and Edward Robinson (New York: Harper & Row, Publishers, 1962).

possible horizon for any understanding whatsoever of Being."[20] *Dasein* (literally, "being-there") can only be understood historically (shades of Dilthey). History is the very way human beings exist rather than something we construct or that in which we live.[21] The meaning of being is concealed in time; to get at being, we must interpret temporality. For Heidegger, the historical being is primary, and it is language that articulates being. It is through language that we have a door onto true or authentic being.

Understanding, in Heidegger's thought, is both the structure of *Dasein* as well as one of the many possible modes of knowing.[22] Hermeneutics is a process of interpreting oneself into existence.[23] Since, for Heidegger, understanding is not a mental but an ontological process, so interpretation is a matter of ontological disclosure. Further, understanding belongs to, and is coextensive with, our existing and, as such, *projects* possibilities for the future. Herein lies Heidegger's unique approach to the famous hermeneutical circle:[24] understanding operates within a relational whole (since understanding never simply proceeds from parts to a whole, but the parts are understood within the context of the whole, and vice versa) that belongs to the very structure of being manifested through phenomena belonging to the horizon of our placement in the world. In other words, understanding is more than a methodologically related cog-

20. Heidegger, *Being and Time*, 1 (italics in original). All page numbers cited from this volume are from this English edition.

21. Heidegger, *Being and Time*, 38–39.

22. Heidegger speaks of potentiality: "Understanding is the existential Being of *Dasein's* own original potentiality-for-Being; and it is so in such a way that this Being discloses in itself what its Being is capable of " (Heidegger, *Being and Time*, 184; original is in italics). For a comparison of the notion of understanding in Schliermacher, Dilthey, and Heidegger, see Palmer, *Hermeneutics*, 130–132.

23. Heidegger actually gives a number of meanings for interpretation, from the *logos* "of the phenomenology of *Dasein*" to methodology (see pp. 61–62). It is not relevant to go into all of these here. Simply put, as Palmer says it, "Hermeneutics, says Heidegger, is that fundamental announcing function through which *Dasein* makes known to himself the nature of being" (*Hermeneutics*, 130).

24. The usual description of the hermeneutical circle is that we are never quite free from presuppositions when we interpret a text. We must understand something of a text (ask the right questions or know where to begin, for example) already before we even begin to interpret it. Thus interpretation is something of a circle.

nitive process; it is the way in which we come to terms with our world.

Even when he turned more explicitly to text interpretation in his later writings, the disclosure of being remained Heidegger's overriding concern, and this was his greatest contribution to the development of hermeneutics. The shift from understanding as an epistemological mode to understanding as an ontological mode is one that set a new course for hermeneutics. Ultimately, it moved the question of truth from a subject-object correspondence (from consciousness to object of consciousness) to "unconcealment."[25] Gadamer's hermeneutics takes up this notion in *Truth and Method*.

4. Hans-Georg Gadamer (1900–). In every sense of the word, Gadamer might be called the "father of philosophical hermeneutics," because he sought to free the human sciences from a methodology based on the natural sciences. He claims that methodological concerns alone cannot do justice to the experience of truth occurring in the humanities. At the same time that he displays methodological misgivings, Gadamer is concerned with the epistemological concerns Heidegger left behind. Although he shows a prejudice for truth over method, he nonetheless did name his seminal work *Truth and Method*[26] rather than *Truth or Method*.

Heidegger's "projections" become Gadamer's "prejudices."[27] These are conditions of understandings whereby in interpretation we have a sense of the whole that comes from tradition and precedes and conditions our understanding of any part[28] (again, the "hermeneutical circle"). This "whole" is the history of a language that conditions understanding and makes it possible. For Gadamer,

---

25. This means that the interpretive process does more than deliver the author's meaning, as Romanticist hermeneutics would have it. Palmer says it well: "When truth is conceived as something which both emerges and plunges back into concealment, when the hermeneutical act places the interpreter on the border of that creative emptiness out of which the work emerged, then interpretation must be creatively open to the as yet unsaid. For 'nothingness' is the creative backdrop of every positive creation; yet this nothingness is meaningful only in the context of being, in its positivity" (*Hermeneutics*, 147).

26. *Truth and Method*, trans. and rev. Josel Weinsheimer and Donald G. Marshall, 2nd rev. ed. (New York: Continuum, 1997).

27. See ibid., 265–271.

28. See ibid., 277–285.

then, hermeneutics is essentially an ontology of language, and understanding is the disclosure of the history of language.[29]

Gadamer contends that all interpretation is an answer to a question, because "the question is implicit in all experience."[30] Questions open up space for new possibilities. To interpret, we must know the question.[31] A hermeneutical understanding of language lies in the fact that every utterance must be understood as an answer to a question. But "the openness of a question is not boundless. It is limited by the horizon of the question."[32]

Gadamer further speaks of interpretation in terms of a "fusion of horizons" between the text and the reader. There is a play between the linguistic dimension (the text) and the historic dimension (the act of reading) in interpretation. Understanding is a process between what is interpreted (the text) and the interpreter (the reader). It is important to note that the two horizons are separate; the hermeneut does not place herself or himself *within* the horizon of the text but interacts with it. This fusion of horizons in interpretation raises the question of temporality.[33] The author of the text and its reader represent different temporalities. This suggests a fusion of present (the history of the interpreter) with tradition (the history of the text). Thus there is no such thing as leaving behind our own history in interpretation; nor does a text have an absolute meaning derived from the historical context in which it was produced.

The interpreter brings certain expectations (projections or prejudices) to a text but finds that these expectations are never totally fulfilled. Rather, the reader expands the horizon of the text because she or he comes to the text from a different historical situation and brings different questions. Thus the hermeneutical circle is hardly a circle but moves the interpretive enterprise forward.[34]

29. See ibid., Part III: "The ontological shift of hermeneutics guided by language," 381–491.

30. Ibid., 362.

31. Cf. ibid., 370.

32. Ibid., 363.

33. Cf. ibid., 306–307.

34. "It might be more accurate to describe Gadamer's phenomenological study of understanding as a hermeneutical spiral rather than a hermeneutical circle" (Roger Lundin, Anthony C. Thiselton, Clarence Walhout, *The Responsibility of Hermeneutics* [Grand Rapids, Mich.: Wm. E. Eerdmans/The Paternoster Press, 1985] 25). Paul Ricoeur also sees a gain in the hermeneutical circle rather than interpretation simply turning back on itself, as we see below, p. 38.

Gadamer is clearly indebted to Heidegger in that he focuses his philosophical hermeneutics on human experience in the world. In this he opens up the world of interpretation further than just involving the humanities and takes on the entire human project. Beyond this, he downplays method in favor of a hermeneutics that concerns itself with understanding as an ontological category.[35] The hermeneut enters into a dialectical relationship with a text by responding to questions posed by the text. Thus, as we said above, all interpretation is answer to questions. The dialectic is between the horizon of the text (tradition) and the horizon of the reader.[36] The key concept here is that the interpreter "belongs" to the text.[37] The questioner is the text, not the reader. This inverts our usual way of thinking, so that the interpreter becomes the "object" and the text is the "subject" posing the questions so that its being can be revealed. It is important to note here that Gadamer does not accept meaning as anything except what is *within* the text, quite independent of the author. The dialectic is between reader and *text*, not between reader and author.

Because Gadamer relegates method to a secondary role, one critique of his philosophical hermeneutics is that there are no criteria for judging an adequate understanding of a text. This critical aspect is taken up by Habermas.

5. Jürgen Habermas (1929–). So far the thinkers we have discussed in the development of modern hermeneutics have all been either theologians or philosophers. Habermas is neither of these; he is a social theorist concerned with a critique of ideologies. In the hermeneutical theories briefly explained thus far, he finds hermeneutics too "universalized," with the critical element lacking. Within dialogue, the interlocutors can "talk past" each other, so that no real understanding occurs. Habermas contends that there must be some kind of "outside" corrective, in the realm of explanation.

Although Gadamer tried to reintroduce epistemological concerns into hermeneutics, he broadened his hermeneutics to the point where critique is impossible. Habermas, on the other hand, focused on issues that interpretation cannot resolve and so reversed the trend toward hermeneutical universality. However, Habermas'

35. Gadamer does not totally disregard method, which is essential in the interpretive process. Method has its proper place, but it cannot deliver truth (see *Truth and Method*, 490–491).

36. See ibid., 460–462.

37. See ibid., 458.

main work has not been in the area of hermeneutics but in social theory, gradually taking on a greater linguistic sensitivity that led him to his theory of communicative action.[38] His critique of hermeneutical theory, as it had developed through to Gadamer, is based on interactions designed to reach consensus.[39] Hermeneutical theory must take into consideration situations where miscommunication takes place.[40]

Habermas would agree with Gadamer that we cannot ignore our own historical place in tradition and that interpretation is essentially a fusion of horizons. While Gadamer is comfortable with placing a method for the human sciences alongside that for the natural sciences, Habermas feels that an adequate hermeneutical theory for the social sciences can ignore neither the scientific methods of the natural sciences nor the linguistic grounding of the hermeneutics of the human sciences.

Habermas enters the hermeneutical discussion at the level of a critique of ideology. It is Ricoeur who takes up this challenge and develops a critical hermeneutics.

38. A good overview of Habermas's thought is provided in William Outhwaite, *Habermas: A Critical Introduction* (Stanford, Calif.: Stanford University Press, 1994).

39. Here we might look ahead to Ricoeur's "conflict of interpretations," his corrective for the same problem of a lack of critical apparatus.

40. See Jürgen Habermas, *The Theory of Communicative Action*, vol. 2: *Lifeworld and System: A Critique of Functionalist Reason*, trans. Thomas McCarthy (Boston: Beacon Press, 1987) 120: "In fact, communicative utterances are always embedded in various world relations at the same time. Communicative action relies on a cooperative process of interpretation in which participants relate simultaneously to something in the objective, the social, and the subjective worlds, even when they *thematically stress only one* of the three components in their utterances. Speaker and hearer use the reference system of the three worlds as an interpretive framework within which they work out their common situation definitions. They do not relate point-blank to something in a world but relativize their utterances against the chance that their validity will be contested by another actor" (italics in the original).

The problem with this critique is that there is a different kind of interpretive process at work between interlocutors (when the validity of a statement can be checked) from that at work between text and reader. Ricoeur addresses this problem when he discusses the movement from discourse to text. For Ricoeur's assessment of the debate between Gadamer and Habermas, see his "Hermeneutics and the Critique of Ideology," in *Hermeneutics and the Human Sciences*, ed. and trans. John B. Thompson (Cambridge: Cambridge University Press, 1981) 63–100.

6. Paul Ricoeur (1913–). Ricoeur's initial philosophical agenda was to write a three-part phenomenology of the will. After completing the first two volumes,[41] he put aside his agenda to write the third volume[42] and began to concentrate more specifically on hermeneutical issues.[43] Ricoeur inherited the rich philosophical hermeneutics of his predecessors and was able to incorporate the benefits of their debates into his own work. He captures both the critical and uncritical aspects of hermeneutics by setting them in dialectical relation. In fact, Ricoeur proceeds dialectically[44] and in this way addresses a number of the hermeneutical problems we have encountered so far in our chronicle of the development of hermeneutics.[45]

Ricoeur holds explanation and understanding in dialectical relationship.[46] By this tactic he resolves the problem of a critique of ideology and capitalizes on both epistemology (to which explanation belongs, a critical moment) and ontology (to which understanding

41. *Fallible Man: Philosophy of the Will,* Part II: *Finitude and Guilt,* Book I: *Fallible Man,* trans. Charles Kelbley (Chicago: Regnery, 1965) and *The Symbolism of Evil,* trans. Emerson Buchanan (Boston: Beacon Press, 1967).

42. This was to be a volume on "thought which starts from the symbol" (*Fallible Man,* Preface, xxi–xxii); see *The Symbolism of Evil,* "Conclusion: The Symbol Gives Rise to Thought," 347–357.

43. Some contend that Ricoeur never did write this third volume. Others would say that his whole hermeneutical undertaking, comprised of many articles and volumes, is the third volume. One way or another, hermeneutics has underscored all Ricoeur's work since the first two volumes appeared.

44. "Dialectic," for Ricoeur, has a very specific meaning: it means relative moments of concrete polarity between two abstract poles that are never erased but remain in dynamic, relative tension with each other. See Paul Ricoeur, *The Philosophy of Paul Ricoeur: An Anthology of His Work,* ed. Charles E. Reagan and David Steward (Boston: Beacon Press, 1978) 150; see also n. 25, p. 48, in my *Liturgy as Language of Faith: A Liturgical Methodology in the Mode of Paul Ricoeur's Textual Hermeneutics* (Lanham, New York, London: University Press of America, 1988).

45. Ricoeur has tended to publish articles rather than systematic works, so delving into his philosophical hermeneutics can be a formidable task. See my *Liturgy as Language of Faith,* chapters 2 and 3, for a summary of his text theory and hermeneutical method. See also Paul Ricoeur, *Interpretation Theory: Discourse and the Surplus of Meaning* (Fort Worth, Tex.: The Texas Christian University Press, 1976); this is not an easy read, but it is a reasonable "introduction" to his text theory and hermeneutical project.

46. Cf. Dilthey, above.

belongs). He also holds in dialectical relationship sense and reference. The sense of a text is "what is said." It is wholly immanent to the language and structure of the text and is recoverable from it by using various explanatory methods. The reference of a text is the world of the text, that "about which" a text is. The reference is about extra-linguistic reality; it has an ontological vehemence. These dialectics "belong" to the text. Additionally, for Ricoeur, other dialectics contribute to the interpretive act.

Ricoeur's textual hermeneutics unfolds in three moments: participation, distanciation, and appropriation.[47] In the moment of participation (a moment of pre-understanding) the interpreter knows herself or himself to belong to a tradition that allows a "guess" at the meaning of a text. Distanciation is an analytical (explanatory) moment that validates the guess. Appropriation (a moment of self-understanding) is choosing from among possible meanings that comprise the world of the text and making a particular meaning our own (and thus becomes part of the world of the interpreter).

In this tripartite method, participation and appropriation are ontological moments, and distanciation is an epistemological moment. Thus the "guess" of the ontological moment of participation stands in dialectical relationship with the analytic, critical moment of distanciation. Herein lies the critique that Habermas finds lacking in Gadamer. Further, the possible meanings opened up in the explanatory analysis of the text are made available to the interpreter, who chooses from among these possibilities and makes one interpretation her or his own (a new self-understanding) in the moment of appropriation.

We see operative here both a fusion of horizons (Gadamer) between the world of the text and the world of the interpreter as well as the hermeneutical circle. But, for Ricoeur, there is always a gain in the hermeneutical circle in that the "guess" of the moment of participation is in dialectical relationship with the world of the text at the explanatory moment, which opens up new possibilities. Something new always happens in interpretation; something is to be gained.

The genius of Ricoeur's methodic textual hermeneutics is that the explanatory moment allows for different methods,[48] so hermeneu-

---

47. These interpretive moments are not to be taken as temporally sequential; they all three stand in dialectical relationship to each other.

48. Such as the traditional historical-critical methods (addressed in Chapter 3) or a post-critical method (addressed in Chapter 4) such as semiotics.

tics has a built-in suspicion. Different agendas on the part of interpreters would have an interpreter choose different explanatory methods to satisfy a specific purpose or to play to the analytic strengths of the interpreter. This means that a text has a wealth of possibilities for interpretation, according to the questions that the interpreter brings. This also suggests that no text has a single, absolute interpretation. There is no "right" interpretation. Ricoeur is not only comfortable with a conflict of interpretations, he promotes it.[49]

With these remarks we conclude our recording of the development of hermeneutics. Obviously, our remarks are necessarily select and incomplete, but they serve our particular purpose. Many, many volumes would need to be written and read in order to do justice to the complexities of thinking that these six figures present. Our particular chronicle focused on those issues—especially understanding— that would help us grasp the importance of hermeneutics for liturgical studies, to which we now turn.

Hermeneutical Issues and Their Import for Liturgical Studies

Since liturgy involves text,[50] it makes sense to say that liturgy involves interpretation. Therefore, hermeneutics is an important discipline for anyone engaged seriously in liturgical studies. Even if not formally involved in hermeneutical theory, all liturgists "interpret" liturgical texts, either formally (theoretically through lectures and publications) or informally (through the practical choices for celebration we might make). We are now in a position to look at some of the specific implications these remarks on hermeneutics have for liturgical studies and praxis.

49. See his *The Conflict of Interpretations: Essays in Hermeneutics,* ed. Don Ihde (Evanston, Ill.: Northwestern University Press, 1974): ". . . every reading of a text always takes place within a community, a tradition, or a living current of thought, all of which display presuppositions and exigencies—regardless of how closely a reading may be tied to the *quid,* to 'that in view of which' the text was written" (p. 3). Ultimately, when there is a conflict of interpretations, the point is not to resolve the conflict in favor of one interpretation or another but to hold the conflicting interpretations in dialectic tension with each other. In this volume Ricoeur brings together such unlikely dialogue partners as psychoanalysis, phenomenology, and religion.

50. See the remarks on p. 19 on liturgy as text in a sacramentary or as text as celebrated. Both kinds of liturgical text are open to interpretation.

We begin with more at-hand issues of praxis and proceed to the more philosophical, methodological ones.

Translations of an Editio Typica

If it is true that all interpretation results in a conflict of interpretations, this raises some interesting questions with respect to the translation of a liturgical *editio typica*.[51] First of all, it must be noted that no text in one language can be rendered exactly equal in another language.[52] Since language discloses being, the different linguistic signs of different languages disclose that being differently. There is rarely a one-to-one equivalent between words in different languages. Add to this the fact that all languages have idiomatic tendencies. Additionally, poetic language is more difficult to translate than everyday language. Further, language is always polyvalent and polysemic;[53] this means that the disclosure of being through language is never total. There is always a "surplus of meaning"[54] that is creative of the language event. To mention one more difficulty, language as symbolic also points to polyvalence on the non-linguistic level as well.[55] With respect to sacred language, a multiplicity of theophanies can be disclosed by the linguistic symbol.

51. An *editio typica* ("typical edition") is a text that has been approved by competent authorities (either by the Congregation for Divine Worship and the Discipline of the Sacraments or by a conference of bishops). It is the basic, official edition of a liturgical text.

52. The Sapir-Whorf hypothesis in American structuralism claims *structural* diversity in languages and it also claims that what is encoded in one system is unique to that system. Any exact translation between languages is impossible. See John Lyons, *Language and Linguistics: An Introduction* (Cambridge: University of Cambridge Press, 1981) 303–312.

53. "By polysemy I shall mean that remarkable feature of words in natural languages which is their ability to mean more than one thing" (Ricoeur, *The Philosophy of Paul Ricoeur*, 120; see also pp. 124 and 126). For Ricoeur, metaphor is the example par excellence of polysemy in communication (see his *Rule of Metaphor: Multi-disciplinary Studies of the Creation of Meaning in Language*, trans. Robert Czerny with Kathleen McLaughlin and John Costello [Toronto, Buffalo, London: University of Toronto Press, 1977]).

54. See Ricoeur, *Interpretation Theory*, 55.

55. See ibid., 53–63. An example of a non-linguistic level Ricoeur gives is in psychoanalysis where the linguistic symbol may be linked to hidden psychic conflicts. An example from the liturgical domain: the laying on of hands may be linked to spiritual healing.

Any attempt to render a translation of an *editio typica* into an absolute equivalent is simply not possible. At best, we have a *dynamic* equivalent. This raises an important question about whether liturgical texts ought not be originally composed in the language in which they are celebrated, using the *editio typica* as a model for the structure of the text. This has the advantage of respecting the tradition of liturgical celebrations (because of the model text) while at the same time respecting the cultural genius of the people and their language.[56]

A different kind of question is raised when we consider the process of translation. No translation begins without presuppositions. These are generally voiced as questions put to the text that guide translators in their work. Questions put to a text include such diverse issues as attempting a more literal or poetic translation, concern with speech cadences, how to render archaic words or objects or cultural situations, and even whether the translation is to be considered definitive or a "work in progress." Depending on the approach to these and other questions, translations by different persons with different concerns might look and sound very differently. At issue here is whether diversity in translation remains faithful to tradition. To put the question another way: Might a conflict of interpretations promote a richness in our encounter with the sacred rather than compromise the truth of tradition?

Although not directly concerned with translation, another issue raised by the polysemy of the linguistic and non-linguistic aspects of symbols is that of the status of the liturgical symbols themselves. Can symbols (e.g., bread) that are relevant in one cultural milieu "speak" in other cultures where they are not relevant or known? If polysemy were not constituent of symbols, this question would necessarily be answered with a negative. The polysemy of symbols, however, opens up space for traditional liturgical symbols to be interpreted meaningfully within a multiplicity of cultures.

For too long the inclusivity issue has been narrowly focused on gender issues. Translations (and originally composed texts) must also take into serious consideration our language about disabilities (e.g., "blind" as an evil), race (e.g., "white" is good and "black" is

56. Obviously, this issue also raises the critically important question of liturgical inculturation, but it would take us too far afield to address this question here. It should be mentioned, too, that some texts are already being originally composed in specific languages. The question we raise really asks whether *all* liturgical texts ought not be originally composed in the language in which they are celebrated.

evil), or generalizations about social or religious classes (all Phari-
sees were against Jesus and were evil).

The polysemy of language and the conflict of interpretations re-
mind us that translation is a never-ending process. As we grow in
our understanding of language use, our texts must be revised to re-
flect that new understanding. Gone are the days when an *editio typica* can be used for centuries with no change. Welcome is the new
era when revision of liturgical texts is an announcement of community growth and vitality with respect to their relationship to the
sacred.[57]

Who Is the Subject of Liturgy?

Another important issue that hermeneutical theory raises is that
of the subject of liturgy.[58] Both Heidegger and Gadamer attack what
is called "subjectism." In this modern tendency, everything is interpreted and exists in terms of the knowing subject (rugged individ-
ualism is a good example of subjectism), who becomes the measure
of all things. Things are only *useful to us.* Interpretation becomes a
creating act, and everything is a projection of the subject who cre-
ates. Without naming it as such, there may be a tendency toward
subjectism in liturgical celebration with distressing consequences,
although they may not usually be perceived as such.

Austin Fleming has made the important distinction between
planning liturgy and *preparing* liturgy.[59] When we plan liturgies, we
run a high risk of falling into subjectism, that is, we tend to shape
liturgy to our own needs. The result is that all too often liturgy loses
its sense of sacredness and becomes a celebration of ourselves. We

57. Actually, there is nothing new in our present practice of a multiplicity
of liturgical texts. We are simply being faithful to Vatican II's desire to go "back
to the sources." No one can contest the presence of a rich diversity of liturgical
texts during the early period of liturgical development, a diversity that still
prevails in the Eastern rites.

58. See my two articles "Liturgical Assembly: Who Is the Subject of
Liturgy?" *Liturgical Ministry* 3 (Spring, 1994) 41–51, and "A Theology of Litur-
gical Assembly: Saints, Relics, and Rites," *Liturgy* 14 (1998) 45–59. See also Mary
Alice Piil, "The Local Church as the Subject of the Action of the Eucharist," in
Peter C. Finn and James M. Schellman, eds., *Shaping English Liturgy: Studies in
Honor of Archbishop Denis Hurley* (Washington: Pastoral Press, 1990) 173–196.

59. Austin Fleming with Victoria Tufano, *Preparing for Liturgy: A Theology
and Spirituality,* rev. ed. (Chicago: Liturgy Training Publications, 1997). See
chapter 2, "Let's Stop Planning Liturgies!"

prepare liturgy by making choices (for the day and season), but those choices are not about us but are about liturgy plunging us into the paschal mystery. Subjectism also rears its head when any element of liturgy takes on the trappings of performance. In all these cases, we are the subject of liturgy with seemingly very little reference to the other. Interpretation always involves a return to the subject, but through the other.

Another area where philosophical hermeneutics may guide us is homiletics. Sometimes the purpose of a homily is given as explaining, applying, or breaking open the Scripture readings for the assembly.[60] The caution here is that interpretation can run the risk of subjectism.[61] On the other hand, if homily is approached as proclamation,[62] then a discourse (not meaning here "dialogue homily") between homilist and assembly ensures that the homily has the nature of disclosure of the divine within the readings. We might raise here the question of truth: Is the homilist simply relating the readings to the lives of the members of the assembly (in which case correctness is a primary concern), or is the homilist aiding the process of the "unconcealment" of the divine as the truth hidden in the proclamation?

Relationship of Language to Being

Perhaps the most important advancement in the development of hermeneutics—as well as the most challenging of the problems—is interest in the relationship of language to being (reality). By the time we come to later philosophical hermeneutics, it is a central issue, especially with Ricoeur. The concern is the facility of language to disclose being and how this occurs. This is hardly a new concern, for it goes all the way back to the Greek philosophers.

Plato recognized a split in reality: there is a hidden reality, belonging to the intelligible order, which is the order of being, and

60. See the *General Instruction of the Roman Missal,* no. 41; also *Inter oecumenici,* no. 54.

61. Subjectism can take different forms in the homily; for example, the homilist can focus on herself or himself (telling stories of oneself, prancing around in the midst of the assembly during the homily, telling jokes just to gain the assembly's attention), the content can be narrowed by the socio-economic status of the majority of the assembly (to the exclusion of others), or be limited to the vision or experience or value judgment of the homilist.

62. For a more extensive treatment of this idea, see my "Homily as Proclamation," *Liturgical Ministry* 1 (1992) 10–16.

there is a sensible reality emerging in dialogue (language). For Plato, language speaks being even though it is hidden. Aristotle asserted that being can be spoken in many ways. Hence there is an inherent ambiguity in the recovery of being that the rules of grammar try to minimalize. These two thinkers represent two distinct philosophical traditions: Plato construed language in the metaphysical realm, whereas Aristotle placed it in the epistemological realm.

In these two great philosophers we see the seeds of a hermeneutical debate that carries through even to today. It was only with Schliermacher that hermeneutics took a decisive step away from being limited to exegesis toward the philosophical realm, where the relationship between epistemology and ontology (explanation and understanding) brings into sharp focus the relationship of language to being.

Ricoeur approaches hermeneutics as a dialectic of explanation and understanding. For him, explanation is the epistemological moment that allows for different, even conflicting methods, and understanding is the ontological moment. In this way Ricoeur transposes the language-being problem from a choice *between* epistemology and ontology to a method that requires both. With this stance we rejoin the Greeks in accepting language as disclosing being.[63] This relationship has enormous consequences for liturgy in both its theoretical domain and its praxis.

If language would have no ontological vehemence, the text, both in its written and celebrated forms, would have no extra-linguistic referent, and so it would have no power to disclose to us the sacred; nor would the celebration of liturgy have the power to transform the members of the assembly by offering a new self-understanding for appropriation; nor would liturgy have any essential bearing on life; nor would liturgy be the communicative bond that effects identity; nor would liturgy be an enactment of the paschal mystery. Without an ontological vehemence, liturgy would at best be a discrete human activity without any assurance of a human-divine encounter.

Liturgy's ontological vehemence places it within a tradition that imposes limits on a specific worshiping community: when shaping a rite for local use, the worshiping community cannot change what

63. For a more complete exposé of this issue, see my entry "Language and Human Experience," in Peter E. Fink, ed., *The New Dictionary of Sacramental Worship* (Collegeville, Minn.: The Liturgical Press, 1990) 644–651.

the rite actually is. In theological terms, for example, there is one Eucharist celebrated by the whole Church. If liturgy discloses, the community cannot impose. The essential structure is a given in the tradition. This leads us to our final reflection.

Relationship of Meaning and Structure

When we say something, what is it that we mean by the saying? Ricoeur defines meaning as the dialectic between sense and reference.[64] This dialectic enables us to make two critical distinctions.

First, since symbol is polyvalent, a "split" sense suggests that we also have a "split" reference.[65] This means that discourse has an innovation of meaning. At one level, every utterance has an obvious (literal) sense with a corresponding (literal) reference. But this sense and reference do not exhaust the meaning of discourse. There is a further, hidden sense and reference. Let us return to our earlier example of Eucharistic bread. A split sense and reference enable us to interpret the Eucharistic bread as something different from the bread made by human hands: it is the Body of Christ. Indeed, all our liturgical symbols find their richness in this hidden (sacred) meaning.

Second, meaning defined as a dialectic of sense and reference says that meaning is dynamic and not limited to cognitive functioning. There can be no "given" meaning but only a disclosed meaning. Each celebration of liturgy, then, is necessarily a different event delivering a different meaning.

The question of how sense and reference are recovered brings us to the issue of structure. Structure is an alliance of composition, genre, and style. It is at hand. Sense and reference are recoverable from a close reading of the structure of a text. Structure is the phenomenon that gives us access to the world of possibilities. In this vein we might distinguish between the "surface" structure of a text that is at hand and the "deep structure" disclosed through interpretation. When we say that liturgy makes present the paschal mystery, we are saying that the paschal mystery is its deep structure. Because the liturgical text is a discrete entity, analysis of its surface structure is possible.[66] Consequently, the liturgical text is an "at hand" tool for

---

64. See, for example, his *Interpretation Theory*, 19–23.

65. See Ricoeur, *The Rule of Metaphor*, 224.

66. This analysis is the moment of explanation or distanciation. It admits of the use of any number of analytical tools. Different analytic tools set the course for

interpreting Christian living, which also has the paschal mystery as its deep structure because of our baptismal commitment. Analysis of Christian living is, at best, only tentative because the whole is never given. Yet, liturgy embodies the whole of the paschal mystery. Its analysis gives us insight into the meaning of our lives.

Conclusion

The development of hermeneutics has spanned over three millennia. In the process we have raised deeper and deeper questions, so that interpretation has more and more at stake. The same is true for the history of liturgical interpretation. No one liturgical era can be said to construct a definitive meaning for liturgy. Liturgical tradition is a history of celebrating communities and their encounters with the divine.

---

of interpretation in different directions, yielding a conflict of interpretations to be arbitrated. Rather than a weakness of the interpretive moment, this conflict points to the richness of the text for delivering many possibilities for appropriation. No one method is a "correct" method; no interpretation is definitive.

It is here that we can revisit the issue we raised in Chapter 1 about whether the written liturgical text can be an appropriate object for interpretation or only the celebration of liturgy itself. The written text has enduring meaning precisely because it is written. The celebration is a fleeting event. Its interpretation is necessarily tentative, until the next celebration. Both objects of interpretation disclose for us the paschal mystery, but each in a different way. Nonetheless, it is the same mystery.

3 Critical Methods

Our brief overview of the development of hermeneutical practice and theory in the last chapter alerts us to the fact that other than philosophers who deal with purely theoretical issues of hermeneutics, virtually all interpretation employs some kind of methodical approach to a text. The art of interpretation always relies on methods. Whether we consider the Greeks and their rhetorical agenda, the early Church writers and their typological agenda, the Scholastics and their theological agenda, the Reformers and their translation programs, the Enlightenment and its challenge to the authority of the Bible, or the modern hermeneuts and their ever more encompassing scope of hermeneutics, throughout we find questions and struggles with method. The plurality of methods suggests that in spite of our propensity to search for *the* meaning of a text, at best the process of interpretation produces only a viable meaning. Differing methods allow us to approach the same text in a number of ways, and each different way delivers a limited layer of meaning.

The strength and weakness of any method can be judged only on the basis of its specified scope and aim. A specific method is chosen to address the corresponding questions put to the text by the interpreter. Different questions, different method. Different exegetical methods address different aspects of a text. Everyone approaches a text with special interests: culture, history, faith, aesthetics, literature, spirituality. The truth of a method (as opposed to an interpretation's disclosure or correspondence with reality—an entirely different question) is measured by its fidelity to its own interpretive rules and the competency of the hermeneut.

As the art of interpretation developed, so did the sophistication of the methods used to interpret various works. Methods have multiplied so rapidly during the modern period of hermeneutics that it is basically impossible for any interpreter to be master of them all. No one interpretation, then, can claim completeness or absolute truth. Modern hermeneutics is an art undertaken by a community of interpreters. Greater sophistication in our application of various methods demands frank and fruitful dialogue among interpreters.[1]

This and the next chapter on hermeneutical methods move this essay into the realm of actual interpretive procedures. When liturgical studies took its rightful place as a specific theological discipline, it shared with biblical studies a common interest in texts. On the one hand, the liturgist might be interested in biblical exegesis, properly speaking, for example in homily preparation. Discerning the meaning of a liturgical proclamation, then, is actually an exercise in biblical exegesis, and we would naturally expect the liturgical hermeneut to use freely the various methods of that discipline. On the other hand, liturgical studies has a wealth of ancient and contemporary liturgical texts ripe for interpretation as texts in their own right apart from biblical texts. It is only natural for liturgical scholars to borrow the tried and true methods of the biblicists. Methodologically speaking, biblical hermeneutics has led the way for liturgical hermeneutics.[2]

It is important to make two more introductory remarks before we take up a description and assessment of the methods that concern this chapter.

First, our discussion of these methods tends to point to liturgical scholars as those who rightfully interpret liturgical texts. This may be true for academic study of those texts, but we may never forget that members of a liturgical assembly are called upon to interpret

1. No method has yet been devised that would have as its scope and aim precisely the arbitration and coordination of conflicting and complementary interpretations of a given text. Such a "macro" hermeneutics would not only deliver the most comprehensive interpretation of a text, but it would also be in a position to point to the areas of a given text that yet need examination. In the case of liturgical texts, such a "macro" interpretation would first of all mediate between the ritual text and the ritual celebration.

2. We see in Chapter 5 how contemporary liturgical hermeneutics is moving in its own direction apart from biblical interpretation because of some of the unique challenges liturgy presents, especially by so many liturgical scholars drawing on the work of Paul Ricoeur.

the liturgical text (celebration) both in terms of an assessment of the liturgical action itself as well as the appropriation of the meaning of that action in their own daily living. We might want to distinguish this latter as an "informal" or "subconscious" interpretation, but it is interpretation nonetheless. If interpretation of liturgical texts is only the work of experts, then the liturgical celebration itself is diminished in power and meaning. This is so because informal interpretation is an essential part of the assembly's participation, leading to appropriation of the transformative action of the mystery being made present.[3] Perhaps like no other text, the liturgical text is a living, celebrated text.[4]

Second, we might categorize methods in several different ways. In this chapter we consider those methods that have traditionally been referred to as "critical," and in the next chapter we consider the "untraditional" or newer "post-critical" methods.[5] I have divided them thus and addressed them in two separate chapters in order to underscore the major methodological shift that has recently taken place. Other divisions for these two chapters might be

---

3. A "macro" interpretation of a liturgical text would consider both the informal and the formal, academic, professional interpretations. Informal interpretation is hardly invalid just because it is, perhaps, less precise and less obvious in application of method. Most of the examples we give are, intentionally, examples of informal interpretation in order to underscore the breadth of the liturgical interpretive process and its implications. One real problem is that the academic community has a built-in critique of its formal interpretations, especially through published dialogues and responses. The celebrating community has little if any built-in critique of its informal interpretations (unless a well-functioning liturgy committee or commission has learned to evaluate and assess regularly). Too often the criterion for a valid informal interpretation is whether a liturgy "works."

4. This opens up the interesting discussion in biblical circles about what, exactly, is the Word of God? Is it the text in the Bible? Or is it the proclaimed, living Word? To the extent that liturgy includes proclamation of Scripture, we might say that liturgy is one of the ways the community incarnates God's Word. Cf. also note 18 in Chapter 1.

5. Not all works on critical methods name them or divide them as I do here (for example, often source criticism and redaction criticism are used interchangeably). I've chosen to present them in this way in order to see more clearly their liturgical application. My purpose is to show the multiple possibilities for interpreting liturgical texts. This has also been the guiding factor, in the best interests of the scope of this essay, for omitting some methods, for example canonical criticism (the reception of a text in a community).

according to "historical" and "literary"[6] or "diachronic" (historical) and "synchronic" (literary). Critical and post-critical are the most mutually exclusive categories. Some of the traditional critical methods, as we will see below, have both diachronic and synchronic aspects that cut across both critical and post-critical methods. Yet these aspects help us understand more clearly what is addressed in the critical methods. So in this chapter we use them to organize the critical methods.

Diachronic, Historical Critical Methods

This group of critical methods is concerned with making a judgment[7] about certain traditional questions the exegete might put to a text: Who wrote it? How did it reach its final edited form? How do we account for textual variants? What is the tradition and context of the text? What is its *Sitz-im-Leben*? Obviously, all these questions point to diachronicity, that is, the development of a text *through* time. Essentially, they are historical questions that cannot be totally severed from the life and situation of the author(s) and editor(s). In other words, the "historical approach presupposes that a literary work carries the imprint of the historical age in which it was produced and that the interpretation of a work is best served by situating it within its historical context and determining the intent of its author."[8] These methods are more directly concerned with recovering the original meaning of a text, so we are alerted to the Romantic authorial preoccupation and all the cautions that requires.

Source Criticism

Source criticism dates to the eighteenth century and addresses authorial questions: Who wrote it? Were there one or several au-

6. See, for example, Steven L. McKenzie and Stephen R. Haynes, eds., *To Each Its Own Meaning: An Introduction to Biblical Criticisms and Their Application* (Louisville, Ky.: Westminster/John Knox Press, 1993). This work includes extensive suggestions for further reading. A very brief and general introduction to exegetical methods is given in John H. Hayes and Carl R. Holladay, *Biblical Exegesis: A Beginner's Handbook,* rev. ed. (Atlanta, Ga.: John Knox Press, 1987). A bibliography at the conclusion of the chapter on each method is quite helpful even for those who are beyond the beginner's stage of exegesis.

7. The "critical" methods derive their name from the Greek verb *krinein,* "to judge."

8. Pauline A. Viviano, "Source Criticism," in McKenzie and Haynes, *To Each Its Own Meaning,* 29.

thors? If an author is assigned, did that person really write it? For example, did Moses write the Pentateuch? Did David write all the psalms? Did Matthew, Mark, Luke, and John write the Gospels? Source criticism uses various literary characteristics to determine the layers of sources in the text. It differs from other literary methods in that its primary aim is to uncover sources. Assuming that individual authors develop a certain consistent style with respect to content, syntax, and vocabulary, textual indicators of different authors at work are noted by inconsistencies or abrupt changes in these areas.

Today's concern with copyright laws and plagiarism is such because we have a much more restricted sense of author as the one who actually pens a work. In former times, the notion of author was much more fluid. Works might be attributed to a well-known individual in order for them to gain credibility. The thought might belong to one person, but the actual writing might be done by a scribe (evidently the case in the Pauline letters). A text might be the product of multiple authorial hands through long development (e.g., the Pentateuch). In the case of liturgy, the text might be that celebrated only by a particular community (e.g., the Gallican liturgy).

The question of an individual author and sources comes up in the study of early liturgical texts (e.g., Christian anaphoras[9]), but it is rarely a question with contemporary texts based on typical editions largely composed by committees. Nevertheless, this does not exclude questions of source criticism from contemporary liturgical texts. For example, a simple perusal of the intercessions from the revised Liturgy of the Hours could identify differing subcommittees that composed them, a judgment based on such factors as inclusive or exclusive language, invocation or petition, length, didactic language, or poetic imagery. Clearly, all these intercessions were not written by a single subcommittee or individual.

A different kind of source-criticism question looms when we consider the inculturation question and typical editions. Translation poses its own problems.[10] A more interesting hermeneutical question concerns author(s) of liturgical texts participating within the culture that celebrates the text. At issue here is the relationship of written text and its ritual celebration or, ultimately, to what extent is

---

9. See, for example, R.C.D. Jasper and G. J. Cuming, eds., *Prayers of the Eucharist: Early and Reformed,* 3rd ed. (New York: Pueblo Publishing Company, 1987).

10. See chapter 2.

the author of a written text also the author of a celebrated text? Is it more correct to say—since each liturgical celebration is a unique language event—that the real author of any liturgical text is the celebrating community? If so, what is the extent of the responsibility of the community itself for the text?

Redaction Criticism

If source criticism shows, generally, that many authors were really at work in the production of sacred texts, redaction criticism shows that the final work has embedded within the text specific interests (theology) of the author. Redaction criticism is closely akin to source criticism. This method is a fairly recent development out of form criticism, which has been especially helpful with respect to analysis of the Gospels. Redaction criticism is concerned with editorial stages, evidenced in different layers of a text. Many times there is little distinction between source and redaction criticism, and rarely are they treated separately.

The redaction critic works with a whole text, not just subunits of the text. Only through the whole can we judge authorial consistency or detect seams and breaks in a text due to later editing. A classic example from the Hebrew Scriptures concerns the J, E, P, and D traditions in the Pentateuch; an example from Christian Scriptures is Paul's second letter to the Corinthians, where we can detect a conflation of several letters by some editor.

Liturgical texts, too, have their redactions. This is true not only for our contemporary committee method of producing the *editio typica*, which undergoes numerous drafts and editing before reaching the final stage of promulgation; it is also true for both later official and improvised "unofficial" redactions. The present revisions of our Sacramentary and Lectionary are a redaction, not a completely new edition of those texts.

The furtive redaction on the part of many lectors of our present Lectionary in order to render the proclamation inclusive is a good example of contemporary liturgical redaction. Another liturgical example of a textual redaction might be a presider who includes his or her personal greeting at the beginning of a liturgy. Each liturgical text has some kind of introductory rite; emendating a personal greeting actually shifts the focus of the rite from God's action to the presider's action. Redaction criticism, far from being mere rubricism, would criticize such emendations because they change the meaning of the text.

Text Criticism

Similar to redaction criticism, text criticism seeks to construct the original wording of a text from a number of extant variants. These variants might be the unintentional result of a scribe's taking a coffee break and then skipping a few words when text copying is resumed. Or variants may be made intentionally by a scribe, for instance when the text is obviously corrupt and the scribe seeks to smooth it over to make sense. Critical translations incorporate what is called a "critical apparatus," which includes all the textual variants, commentary, dating, and an educated guess as to what is the original wording.

Liturgical texts may have their unintentional or intentional variants, especially in their celebration. Unintentional variants might be simple slips of the tongue, similar to what might happen during any public speaking. Intentional variants are more serious. Some have become rather common. For example, some presiders change "The Lord *be* with you" to "The Lord *is* with you." This may seem like an inconsequential variant, but a text critic could show how this actually changes the meaning and purpose of the text. The verb "be" is the present subjunctive optative mood; that is, it expresses a wish. Here it functions clearly as a greeting.[11] The verb "is," the present indicative mood, expresses simple statement of fact, which does not function as a greeting.[12] In this example, the variant actually changes the purpose of the action. Another example: presiders sometimes change the words of blessing from "bless *you*" to "bless *us*." The interpretation suggests a desire on the part of the presider to include

11. The rubrical note in the Sacramentary indicates that the presider extends his or her hands during this greeting. A hermeneutical activity is the determination of how that gesture is performed; reaching out to the assembly with the body slightly leaning forward would be a natural gesture. This is a different interpretation of "with extended hands" from, say, the rubrical note during the opening prayer, where the gesture is the *orans* position (hands extended with palms lifted upward). These few examples demonstrate that interpretive activity occurs throughout liturgical celebration.

The example of the grammar of "The Lord be with you" also reminds us that rarely does an exegete work only within one method. In this example, grammatical criticism (see below) is also at work. The various critical methods overlap, as we noted in our discussion of source criticism.

12. Cf. Thomas S. Krosnicki, "Grace and Peace: Greeting the Assembly," in *Shaping English Liturgy: Studies in Honor of Archbishop Denis Hurley,* ed. Peter C. Finn and James M. Schellman (Washington: The Pastoral Press, 1990) 96–97.

himself or herself as part of the assembly. At the same time, this variant also changes the nature of the presider's role of leading the assembly and, therefore, of doing some actions explicitly as the one who stands at the front of the assembly *in persona Christi.*

Conscious textual variants introduced into the celebration of a liturgical ritual are always a hermeneutical activity. They cannot be undertaken lightly, because they more or less change the speech act.

Tradition Criticism

Tradition criticism also addresses text origins by attempting to identify the growth and development of the tradition that gave rise to the text. Many ancient texts had an oral tradition in place before the text was committed to written form. This is true for much of the Hebrew and Christian Scriptures. It is no less true for much of the content of our liturgical texts. An interesting case at point is the injunction in the *Didache* to let the prophets pray as they will,[13] suggesting the existence of an oral tradition alongside the beginnings of written texts.

Tradition criticism implies a passing on of oral material through successive generations of a community. Sometimes this material is attributed to a specific individual (e.g., the proverbs of Solomon), but more likely they are really anonymous compositions shaped by the re-telling over generations. Thus tradition criticism is concerned with both the content and process of text composition.

Since liturgy is a unique combination of written text and oral performance, it always has an oral tradition that continually shapes the revision of texts. Moreover, numerous rubrical indications to use "these or similar words" intimate an oral tradition at work even in our contemporary times. Liturgy always has its play between the transmission of "exact wording" and its oral tradition of celebrations.

Historical Criticism

Sometimes "historical criticism" is the name given to a whole block of critical methods because every text that is produced in some enduring form is produced in some historical context, and that context conditions the final content. This method functions in its own right when historical context is the focal point of the inter-

---

13. *Didache* 10:7. This passage is generally accepted to refer to the Eucharist but may only refer to a meal blessing. In either case, a prayer text is given with obvious reference to an oral tradition.

pretation. For example, knowing that a psalm is pre-exilic (e.g., Ps 110), exilic (e.g., Ps 137), or post-exilic (e.g., 147) affects how we understand the psalm. In the study of early Christian anaphoras, knowing to which "family" an anaphora belongs alerts us to certain structural expectations.[14] We know that Eucharistic Prayer I sounds very different from Eucharistic Prayer IV because they derive from Western and Eastern contexts, respectively.

Perhaps an example of historical criticism at work in contemporary liturgies is the practical choice of hymns for use at liturgy. Are children's songs that were composed primarily for catechetical purposes ever appropriate for liturgical use? What happens when we incorporate these songs into our liturgies? Another example: Some Roman Catholics object to singing hymns composed by, for example, Luther or the Wesleys. Yet, as ecumenical discussions uncover more similarities than differences with the Reformation churches, we might rightly judge that the theological context is very similar, if not identical, to what we might subscribe today.

Form Criticism

As the name implies, form criticism is concerned with the form, content, and function of a unit or subunit and how they are related in order to determine meaning. Thus one major task of the form critic is to "cut" (divide) larger texts into units and subunits. Further, the form critic is interested in how the units or subunits fit into the larger whole to make a cohesive work. It is "integrative pattern analysis."[15] Form criticism is a synchronic method to the extent that it looks to a text for literary forms. However, the discernment of patterns shared with other texts marks this method as diachronic, and so we include it here among the diachronic methods. This method also reminds us of the interrelationship of biblical data.

It is the form critic who recognizes the differences and consequent significance of the enthronement psalms, for example, from the historical psalms. A form critic would also be interested, for example, in whether Jesus' Supper discourse with his disciples

14. Cf. Louis Bouyer, *Eucharist: Theology and Spirituality of the Eucharistic Prayer,* trans. Charles Underhill Quinn (Notre Dame, Ind.: University of Notre Dame Press, 1968) esp. 136–186. Liturgists have become much more sophisticated in their discussion of early anaphoras, but Bouyer's work remains a classic.

15. Martin J. Buss, "Form Criticism," in McKenzie and Haynes, *To Each Its Own Meaning,* 70.

shares the characteristics of a typical farewell speech from that historical period of its formation.

A liturgist who is essentially working as a form critic would be interested in how the major divisions of a ritual are cut[16] or in differentiating narrative sections of the Eucharist (e.g., parts of the Eucharistic Prayer) from pure praise prayers (e.g., the *Gloria*). The form-critical liturgist would also be interested in the structure of the presidential prayers or the structure of the general intercessions. Concerning the latter, for example, we might ask, "Is a silence after the announcement of the intention allowing for prayer a structural requirement of the prayer?" or "Is 'We pray to the Lord; Lord, hear our prayer' sufficient for intercessory *prayer*?"

Synchronic, Literary Critical Methods

All the methods we have considered so far concern extra-textual, temporally bound, historical aspects of interpretation. Now we turn to a very different kind of approach whereby we focus on aspects wholly *within* the text. Synchronic critical methods are more literary in type; they are concerned with the text's language and language use.

Literary Criticism

This is a generic term overlapping with other methods (e.g., rhetorical criticism). Composition, structure, style, and mood are all concerns of the literary critic. Here, cutting the text into units and subunits is also important as an aid for separating the layers of a text by its content or its literary characteristics. Literary criticism, as synchronic, simply examines a text *qua* text for its literary characteristics. For example, a literary critic would ask of Psalm 110, "How did we get from the majestic enthronement of the first oracle to the imprecation of the second?"[17] It is the literary critic who would look

16. A form critic, for example, might raise the question about whether the presentation of the gifts and preparation of the altar are part of the Liturgy of the Eucharist or a preamble to it. Or, with respect to the Liturgy of the Hours, does the Scripture reading form a separate part of the rite from the psalmody (with the consequence that the Gospel canticles are also separated from the psalmody rather than alternately understood as their doxological climax)?

17. Psalm 110 is an important one in the revised Liturgy of the Hours, occurring on all four Sundays at Evening Prayer II as well as on many feasts. Interestingly enough, the revised rite omits verse 6, but one can legitimately ask

for changes in vocabulary and style to determine which of the thirteen letters traditionally ascribed to Paul are authentic and which probably come from a Pauline school.

Applying literary criticism to a liturgical text might raise a question about how the three acclamations included in the Eucharistic Prayers cut the text. If we add more acclamations (for example, in the children's Eucharistic Prayers), how does that affect the narrativity and integrity of the prayer? Or a literary critic might wonder about the liturgical appropriateness of using the Nicene Creed, which is largely apologetic and doctrinal in content, as opposed to the use of the baptismal creed with its question/response format or the Apostles' Creed, which is the more ancient statement of our faith.

Rhetorical Criticism

Sometimes rhetorical criticism is considered a subdivision of literary criticism, for they both deal with literary characteristics of the text and cutting it into appropriate units and subunits. However, as the name implies, rhetorical criticism is particularly concerned with the art of convincing or persuading. Rhetorical criticism is a "search for effective communication" that "invites a specific literary method that will enable the critic systematically to study the discourse's strategy and techniques of effective communication."[18] In this sense, rhetorical criticism is also diachronic, for it is interested in what the author wished or intended. Moreover, it is interested in the reader (the first method we have considered so far to be so), since it is looking for effects of the text on its reader. The prophetic literature of the Hebrew Scriptures has a great deal of material of special interest to the rhetorical critic. Uncovering the preponderance of parenetic material in Paul's letters is the work of a rhetorical critic.

A liturgist could research homiletic vocabulary and elements for rhetorical import. Or the liturgist might approach the sign of the cross at the beginning and end of liturgy as an *inclusio* (an element of literary criticism) and inquire how this affects our grasp of the integrity of the single communicative action that unfolds between them.

---

what violence does that omission do to the meaning of the psalm itself? The revised rite also omits three imprecatory psalms altogether: Psalms 58, 83, and 109.

18. Yehoshua Gitay, "Rhetorical Criticism," in McKenzie and Haynes, *To Each Its Own Meaning*, 135–136.

Grammatical Criticism

Words, sentences, language, syntax, and grammar are all the domain of the grammatical critic. This method is perhaps the most synchronic of all, for its inquiry is most clearly limited to the text itself. For example, the grammatical critic would be interested in counting word occurrences: how often does the Hebrew word *zkr* ("memory," "to remember") occur in Deuteronomy[19] or in the psalms? Grammatical criticism would help us to know that Luke-Acts is a composite because of the similar vocabulary and syntax.

Recently a participant at a liturgical education program asked why a few places in the Eucharistic liturgy revert to the first person singular pronoun, as before communion with the "Lord, *I* am not worthy . . . ," when almost all other texts are communitarian (first person plural). Unbeknownst to her, she was asking a grammatical critic's question. We are also engaged in grammatical criticism when we know that liturgical terms such as "sacrifice," "memory," or "offering" have more specific liturgical meaning than when we use these terms in our everyday language.

Gains and Limits of the Critical Methods

All these methods overlap. Some are used more than others. Some are more encompassing than others. It is good to recall here Gadamer's break with the desire to find a method for the human sciences that parallels the exactitude and certitude claimed of the methods of the physical sciences. In point of fact, exactitude and certitude in the human sciences simply cannot exist. At best, we can more or less validate reasonable guesses.

That does not mean, of course, that searching for better methodological procedures for the human sciences is a moot exercise. Quite the contrary. Much knowledge can be gained by the use of the critical methods. We just cannot look for definitive agreement about definitive meanings of texts. We can expect debates over composition and content of texts. Rather than being a deficit, this simply points to the richness of sacred texts and the interpretive challenge meted out by meanings that are inexhaustible. Obviously, we have made

19. For its liturgical implications, see my study "Concern for Others: *Remembering*," in *Liturgy as Living Faith: A Liturgical Spirituality* (Scranton, Pa.: University of Scranton Press; London and Toronto: Associated University Presses, 1993) 5–17.

no attempt to present extensive analyses of these methods. Enough is given, hopefully, to see the critical methods as indispensable for liturgists as they are for biblicists.

Until very recently, all professional liturgists researched texts using the critical methods. We only need recall the textual work on Eucharist by Bouyer, Jungmann, and Dix; the work on the liturgical year by Talley; and the study of the Liturgy of the Hours by Taft, to mention but a few. Enormous strides in understanding the liturgy have been made, thanks to the number and richness of liturgical texts we have available for analysis and the tried and true methods made available to us by biblical scholars. Add to this the fact that many liturgists came to these studies via Scripture studies (Lucien Deiss immediately comes to mind), and it is no wonder that we liturgists were formed in and still use the critical methods.

The questions guiding the biblical exegete also guide the liturgical exegete. We are interested in how the liturgical texts were formed, how and why they differed from region to region, what theologies of liturgy might be gleaned from the texts. We learn about the origins of rites and feasts. We learn about what once was and now is no more (e.g., the popularity of Ember Days). We discover that some of what we now do and seems new is really an ancient part of liturgy (e.g., communion from the cup). We learn that some developments are relatively recent (e.g., kneeling during the Eucharistic Prayer).

As liturgical studies came into its own as a theological/pastoral discipline, liturgists were fortunate to have methods available for use. We gained by the trials and errors of our biblical colleagues. We plunged into our discipline with all the energy of those who know where they are going and what they want to accomplish. We rediscovered and reemphasized long-forgotten liturgies (e.g., the work of Baumstark, Mateos, and Storey in popularizing "cathedral" morning and evening prayer). We sorted out what was devotional and what pertained to the authentic tradition of liturgical prayer. We discarded or minimalized aspects of liturgy that underscored a context-sensitive practice or theology no longer appropriate (e.g., bells during Eucharist).

We have hardly exhausted all the critical research on liturgical texts. Students of liturgy will no doubt still be formed in these methods. A new methodological mood is beginning to take place, however, and this because the renewal of Vatican II has brought us to ask different questions of the liturgy that these traditional methods cannot address. For example, critical studies can demonstrate the relationship of liturgy and life. Recently this relationship has taken on a new urgency and has pushed the methodological limits. Critical studies can point to paradigmatic elements of rites, but they are stretched beyond capacity when we try to respond to questions of inculturation. Critical studies can respond to historical and authorial questions, but they must be silent when we ask questions deriving from the advances in, say, communications (what is the nature of the dialogue between homilist and assembly?) or architecture (what is our spatial perception of community?).

New questions demand new methods. Once again, liturgists have been fortunate to have professional colleagues in other disciplines break ground upon which we can capitalize for our own efforts. The newer methods being employed by some liturgists today are borrowed largely from the literary critics and are often referred to as post-critical methods. To these we now turn.

4 Post-critical Methods

Critical methods are indispensable for an appreciation of the composition and content of texts. Yet, as we saw in the last chapter, these methods are limited. Especially in recent decades new questions have been put to biblical and liturgical texts, questions that stretch interpreters beyond what the critical methods can deliver. Thus was born what we term "post-critical methods." These take their place alongside the critical methods; they do not replace them. Unlike the critical methods, many of which originated with exegesis of sacred texts, the post-critical methods find their origins among literary critics and have been borrowed by exegetes of sacred tests.

Most of the critical methods have been used by liturgists, especially when interpreting ancient texts. This is not equally true of the post-critical methods. Some of these hardly apply to liturgical texts, or liturgists have yet to ask the questions that would entail use of some of these methods. Accordingly, this chapter only briefly mentions those methods that have not figured prominently among liturgists. Some methods are not immediately applicable to liturgy and so are omitted altogether.[1] This chapter, in other words, tries to give an overview of post-critical methods, paying special attention to those with liturgical import, without attempting to be exhaustive.

---

1. For example, Noam Chomsky's generative grammar. For those interested, see his *Current Issues in Linguistic Theory* (New York: Humanities Press, 1964).

Linguistic Turn

The beginning of this century witnessed an important linguistic turn. By the last half of this century, linguistics seems to dominate hermeneutics. Thus we find a host of new methods developing.

Structural Linguistics

Ferdinand de Saussure (1857–1913) taught linguistics of particular languages and the history of linguistics. In 1916 his *Course in General Linguistics,* based on lecture notes, was published posthumously. De Saussure is considered a structuralist, but in a more general sense than we consider below. Certain linguistic stances he took are characteristic of structuralism, no matter what the school.

For de Saussure, the linguistic sign is not the representative of a preexisting idea or thing (as in Augustine, for example, where a sign points to something beyond itself), but rather a sign is based on differences within the linguistic system. The sign is a union of a concept and a sound pattern, the signified and signifier. His emphasis is on structure as a system of differences. "The important point to note here, and it is essential for the understanding of Saussurean structuralism, is that the sign is not a meaningful form: it is a composite entity which results from the imposition of structure on two kinds of substance by the combinatorial and contrastive relations of the language system."[2] Meaning, then, is that which is systematically produced by following certain rules of the language and does not exist apart from the linguistic forms. For example, we know

---

2. John Lyons, *Language and Linguistics: An Introduction* (Cambridge: Cambridge University Press, 1981) 221. De Saussure's distinction between signifier and signified allows for the study of the signifier apart from the signified; the form of the sign is the signifying relationship. The Danish linguist Louis Hjelmslev broadened the notion of form to apply to both parts of the sign; hence the form of the signifier and the form of the signified (see Louis Hjelmslev, *Prolegomena to a Theory of Language,* trans. Francis J. Whitfield [Madison, Wis.: The University of Wisconsin Press, 1956] 58). Hjelmslev substitutes the terms "expression" and "content" for signifier and signified, respectively (cf. 47–60). He wants to move away from using sign as "a stock of labels fastened on pre-existent things" (58). Further, all "terminology is arbitrary, and consequently nothing prevents us from using the word *sign* as a special name for the expression-form (or, if we wished, for the expression-substance, but this would be both absurd and unnecessary). But it appears more appropriate to use the word *sign* as the name for the unit consisting of content-form and expression-form and established by the solidarity that we have called the sign function" (58).

what "red" is, not because we have seen and eaten a red apple, but because we know red is not[3] blue or green or any other color.

Another important distinction in de Saussure is between *la langue*, which is the system of linguistic signs (such as the words in what we conventionally understand as language) or codes governing linguistic events, and *la parole*, which is a particular occurrence of language (such as discourse or conversation). De Saussure's point is that the whole *(la parole)* is greater than the sum of its parts *(la langue)*.

Although de Saussure proposed a wholly synchronic approach to language, he also recognized that there can be no absolute, context-free meaning. Languages are social facts: " . . . they are different from, though no less real than, material objects; . . . they are external to the individual and make him [or her] subject to their constraining force; . . . they are systems of values maintained by social convention."[4] Some signs are "natural signs" (for example, smoke signifies fire and clouds signify rain), but most are conventional; that is, social convention and use assign a signifier to a signified. Thus his principle of the arbitrariness of linguistic signs.

One of the most potent critiques of de Saussure regards his insistence on the synchronicity of the linguistic system. If language is only turned in on itself, of what value is meaning? What can language really say? Applied to liturgy, de Saussure can alert us to seek meaning in the whole rather than in any individual element. But ultimately we would look outside the language system for an ontological vehemence. Nevertheless, de Saussure opened a door for different schools of structuralism and semiotics, and their methods can be very valuable for liturgical studies.

Formalism

Admittedly dependent on de Saussure and his tenets, formalism has its roots in Russia with linguists like Roman Jakobson, Vladimir Propp, and Jan Mukařovský. With proponents like Carnap, it has affinities with the analytic philosophy school. Eventually, with the Prague School, it devolved into functionalism.[5]

3. Here the "not" means "is in opposition to."
4. Lyons, *Language and Linguistics*, 221.
5. The Prague School has origins in the émigré Jakobson and the Prague Linguistic Circle. Lyons sees functionalism in linguistics as a "particular movement within structuralism" (ibid., 224).

Formalism is concerned with the opposition of structure to form. Structure makes available the mode or function (e.g., communicative, religious, aesthetic) of the linguistic text. Underlying this structure is the form, an absolute rather than a relational entity. A linguistic analysis of the structure (function) of a text[6] leads the interpreter to the form. Keep in mind, however, that form is delivered up by the linguistic code of the text as structured; the meaning never moves outside of the text. Formalism admits of no extra-linguistic reality. The formalist school wishes "to rehabilitate the particular text as the primary object of interpretation."[7] It is this independence of a text that allows it to function differently in different contexts.

Liturgical hermeneuts realize that the interpretation of a liturgical text can never remain tied to or within the text itself. Nevertheless, formalism, especially in its functional aspects, can be an aid to liturgical hermeneuts. For example, how the acclamations function in the liturgy would be a question of interest to the functional linguist. Some of the narrative methods of the formalist school are helpful for analyzing the narrative texts of liturgy.[8]

Structuralism and Semiotics

Dating from the 1950s and 1960s in France, structuralism has its roots in formalism. We might describe structuralism as the analysis of structures (e.g., narrativity) that make possible the study of various kinds of human activities.[9] Semiotics is the study of sign systems. It asks the question "What holds the text together?"[10] Semiotics, then, is a particular kind of rule-governed analysis which a struc-

6. The texts these linguists work with are largely narratives.

7. Werner G. Jeanrond, *Theological Hermeneutics: Development and Significance* (New York: Crossroad, 1991) 102.

8. For further applications, see chapters 4 and 5 of my *Liturgy as Language of Faith: A Liturgical Methodology in the Mode of Paul Ricoeur's Textual Hermeneutics* (Lanham, New York, London: University Press of America, 1988) and especially pp. 104–120 on Jakobson's communication factors and functions.

9. For example, Greimas practices semiotics, Lévi-Strauss is interested in structural anthropology, and Barthes pursues literary criticism.

10. Walter Vogels, *Reading and Preaching the Bible: A New Semiotic Approach*, Background Books 4 (Wilmington, Del.: Michael Glazier, 1986) 19. Part 1, "Theory and Methodology," is a very fine, simple introduction to semiotics and how it might actually be used by someone not a professional semiotician.

turalist might use and which has been helpful for both biblicist and liturgist alike.

Structuralism begins with the premise that "all social activity is governed by abstract conventions, convictions, and rules."[11] These patterns of activity are encoded in texts[12] that mirror both surface and deep structures. The surface structure of a text is that which is easily perceived and, therefore, able to be analyzed, for example, the actants or the plot. The deep structure[13] is the complex structure that consists of the ordering principles or the rules that generate the structural patterns.

From these brief introductory remarks certain characteristics of structuralism can be noted.

1) Structuralism only addresses the text in its final form; it is not interested in its authorial intent, historical setting, or development. Even in the case of text variants, the structuralist simply analyzes the text at hand, ignoring variants in other versions of the text.

2) The text is given in a language that is any set of ordered symbols through which meaning is delivered. Like text, language cannot be limited to mean spoken English or Latin, for example. Social behavior has a language, that is, rules that are followed. Another example from a previous era makes the point: when the pastor walked into a Catholic elementary school classroom and the students immediately rose to their feet and sang out in unison, "Good morning, Father!" this behavior expressed the "language" of being a Catholic elementary school student.

11. John H. Hayes and Carl R. Holladay, *Biblical Exegesis: A Beginner's Handbook*, rev. ed. (Atlanta, Ga: John Knox Press, 1987) 111.

12. Text does not necessarily mean written text, although much of structural analysis focuses on written texts, especially narratives. In a paper entitled "Introduction to the Semiotics of Liturgy" and distributed to the Ritual-Language-Action: Social Sciences Study Group of the North American Academy of Liturgy during its meeting in Nashville (2–5 January 1990), the late Mark Searle proposed that "semiotics offers a single, consistent, rigorous and coherent method for analyzing all the different codifications of the rite. Using the same method, one can analyze written texts, movement and gesture, music, the use of space, architecture" (1–2).

13. The reader is cautioned against understanding surface structure as "superficial" and deep structure as "significant, challenging." These terms have a very specific meaning in structuralism.

3) The referent is not equal to the deep structure, because structuralism is synchronic; it brackets any extra-textual reference.

4) Perhaps the most important feature of structuralism is that it follows the principle of binary opposites.[14] This principle states that our thinking and social activities are captured in categories of opposites. We know one entity because we know the meaning of its opposite. For example, rich has meaning in opposition to poor, sick in opposition to healthy, life in opposition to death. Liturgically speaking, some binary opposites are human and divine, bread and consecrated host.

Semiotics as Method and an Assessment

Semiotics is gaining ground as a helpful method for scriptural exegesis; it is becoming important in liturgical studies as well.[15] We take a more extensive look at semiotics because of its continued promise for liturgical studies.[16]

---

14. The importance of these binary opposites is eminently clear when we examine structural methods. Perhaps the methodology most dependent on this principle of binary opposites is semiotics, especially evident in the semiotic square. The use of binary opposites is one area where Paul Ricoeur shows his sympathy with French structuralism. However, Ricoeur goes one step further when he sets the binary opposites in a *dialectical* relationship (e.g., explanation and understanding, sense and reference, event and meaning).

Some critics of Ricoeur seem to pass over dialectics as the real key to understanding him. See, for example, Jeanrond's critique in *Theological Hermeneutics,* 75–76; see also his *Text and Interpretation as Categories of Theological Thinking,* trans. Thomas J. Wilson (New York: Crossroad, 1988) and J. Michael Joncas's use of Jeanrond in his critique of my *Liturgy as Language of Faith* in his article "Joyce Ann Zimmerman's 'Text Hermeneutics' Approach to Liturgical Studies: A Review and Some Methodological Reflections," *Questions Liturgiques: Studies in Liturgy* 74 (1993) 208–220. See also my review of James Fodor, *Christian Hermeneutics: Paul Ricoeur and the Refiguring of Theology* (Oxford: Clarendon Press, 1995) in the *International Philosophical Quarterly* 38 (1998) 86–88.

15. Walter Vogels remarks, in assessing the state of biblical exegesis used by homilists, that the historical-critical methods are "very technical" ones, "requiring a high degree of specialization and thus making it less accessible for the Bible-reader and for the pastor" (*Reading and Preaching the Bible,* 25). In chapter 2 Vogels explains why semiotics is a more accessible method for the nonprofessional exegete.

16. Chapter 5 examines those liturgists using semiotics as a method of text interpretation.

One important advance of semiotics over structuralism is semiotics' interest in transformations (e.g., from good to bad or from poor to rich). The entire method proceeds by means of uncovering oppositions and transformations. The "generative trajectory" is the analytical model semioticians (following A. J. Greimas) use to expose the deep and surface structures. The analysis takes into account structures at three levels: (1) semiotic structures that are the deep level;[17] (2) the narrative structures that are the surface level;[18] and (3) the discursive structures.[19] Further, the narrative and discursive structures have "a semantic dimension [that] contains the units of meaning, while the syntactic dimension consists of the rules governing the organization and transformation of meaning at each level."[20] The actual analysis involves first cutting the text (Vogels' terminology) or segmenting the text (Searle's terminology), constructing the semiotic square (a series of contrary and contradictory relations that is the deep structure) and doing the semantic and syntactic analyses of the narrative and discursive structures.[21]

Semiotics tries to make explicit those operations that a reader of a text performs more or less unconsciously. However, this explication remains solely an exercise realized on a text *qua* text; that is, it is synchronic, immanent to the text itself. Herein lies semiotics' strength and its weakness.

Approaching a text *qua* text is a strength because it enables the hermeneut to engage in an interpretive process that is wholly

17. In order to keep his method relatively simple, Vogels does not address this level of analysis. He discusses the semiotic square after his notes on the narrative and discursive analyses in terms of the link between these two analyses (see Vogels, *Reading and Preaching the Bible*, 64–67; see also Searle, "Introduction to the Semiotics of Liturgy," 14–16).

18. See Vogels, *Reading and Preaching the Bible*, 47–57; also Searle, "Introduction to the Semiotics of Liturgy," 16–18.

19. See Vogels, *Reading and Preaching the Bible*, 57–64; also Searle, "Introduction to the Semiotics of Liturgy," 18–20. Searle calls the discursive structures the "discoursive" structures.

20. Searle, "Introduction to the Semiotics of Liturgy," 14. Vogels does not make this distinction between the semantic and syntactic dimensions in his analyses.

21. Part 2, "Practical Exercises" of Vogels' *Reading and Preaching the Bible* takes the reader through some sample analyses of scriptural texts. Pages 28ff. of Searle's paper take the reader through an analysis of the marriage rite, the blessing of water, and an example of semiotics applied to the analysis of the architecture of a church building.

scientific, paralleling a rigor and lending an objectivity with respect to the data such as has been possible thus far only with the methods of the physical sciences.[22] The effect of this gained methodological objectivity is that text itself takes on a new status. Text is valued not as a door through which we might gain access to the intention(s) of the text producers, their culture or historical context, or how the text came to be; nor is text valued for the effects it may have on the current text users. Rather, text is valued because an inherent dynamic lies within the text, the exposure of which is a worthy project in itself. A text contains its own credibility, its own world, its own life. Semiotics eminently respects this autonomy.

Semiotics' strengths are, ironically, also its major weaknesses. Semiotics sets aside—"brackets," to use phenomenological terminology—questions about extra-textual ontological reality in order to focus on the text itself and what it says. Yet, every text has an engagement with its reader(s) and, as document of life, it contains traces of lived experience.[23] The extra-textual ontological vehemence here is not the same as that of the critical methods that seek to understand a text in terms of the context that produced it; rather, we are concerned with the extra-textual in terms of the text's engagement with its current reader(s), admittedly introducing a diachronic aspect to the discussion. We annotate this position in the next three paragraphs.

A semiotic analysis cannot account for creation or innovation of meaning, yet in fact this is part and parcel of hermeneutics. Paul Ricoeur suggests that the discontinuity of discourses—shifting from an analytic, scientific discourse to a speculative, philosophical discourse—is the only way to account for innovation in language use.[24] The ontological implications of a text are underscored in this shift of discourses, where meaning is located in the polyvalence of the text's sense and reference.

22. This was the enduring concern in the development of modern hermeneutics that we outlined in chapter 2 above.

23. Refer to my comments on Ricoeur's textual hermeneutics in chapter 1.

24. See Paul Ricoeur, "Metaphor and Philosophical Discourse," in *The Rule of Metaphor: Multi-disciplinary Studies of the Creation of Meaning in Language,* trans. Robert Czerny with Kathleen McLaughlin and John Costello (Toronto, Buffalo, London: University of Toronto Press, 1977) 257–313, especially pp. 295–303. Especially note his comment that we must "abandon the naïve thesis that the semantics of metaphorical utterance contains ready-made an immediate ontology . . ." (p. 295). For a summary of this discussion, see my *Liturgy as Language of Faith,* 55–58.

It might be helpful at this point to clarify the term "meaning" for this context. For semiotics, meaning is immanent to a text and is determined by the system of relations (oppositions) of the signs that comprise the text as a whole. For Ricoeur, this is only one part of meaning, what he calls the sense of the text. Linguistically, the sense of a text is *what is said*,[25] the surface structure of a text that certainly may be analyzed according to any synchronic method, such as semiotics.[26] But this is not all a text is; in addition to sense, there is reference that "is uncovered in the depth-meaning of language in use and it points to extra-linguistic reality."[27] Reference bears the ontological vehemence of a text as the "world" of discourse, the "about which" proper to a text. Text has both a surface structure that is its organization and a deep structure that is its recoverable trace of human activity. Meaning, for Ricoeur, is a dialectic between sense and reference, between linguistic structure and life structure. Further, in particular kinds of discourse (Ricoeur draws heavily on poetic discourse), there is a "split" sense and reference, as previously noted. That is, one level of the sense—the literal—delivers up an obvious reference, but a second, only implied sense opens up an innovative world of reference.[28]

Being comes before saying. For Ricoeur, interpretation always entails a return to the subject; language always indicates self-reference.[29] With this statement we come to realize the implications of interpretation as the intersection of the world of the text and the world of the hermeneut. Thus, while semiotics is an analysis that is wholly immanent to the text and is important to the interpretive process, interpretation cannot remain there.[30]

25. For semiotics, the *what is said* is the *how it is said*.
26. Ricoeur recognizes the limits of semiotics (indeed, any method): "The consciousness of the validity of a method . . . is inseparable from the consciousness of its limits" ("Structure and Hermeneutics," in *The Conflict of Interpretations: Essays in Hermeneutics,* ed. Don Ihde [Evanston, Ill.: Northwestern University Press, 1974] 44). At the same time he recognizes that method is an indispensable hermeneutical moment: "I do not say that they [symbols and myths] do not lend themselves to the structural method; I am even convinced to the contrary. I say that the structural method does not exhaust their meaning . . . " ("Structure and Hermeneutics," 47).
27. Zimmerman, *Liturgy as Language of Faith,* 55.
28. See ibid., 57.
29. See ibid., 58–61.
30. At least not if the interpretation is to be more than an academic exercise. Obviously, my concern to reinsert method into a larger hermeneutical framework having an ontological vehemence is colored by my liturgical interests.

Beyond Structuralism

Structuralism and its many schools came into their own during the twentieth century as a "corrective" to the Romantic tendencies of the critical methods. Another movement arising in the latter part of this century that critiques and goes beyond structuralism is "poststructuralism." The poststructuralist schools share certain tenets with structuralism: there is nothing outside the text, no ontology recoverable in a text, and a text has its own authority. At the same time, poststructuralism critiques structuralism: there are no universals in the deep structure of a text, no strict objectivity; a text cannot be simply atemporal, and a discipline cannot be so self-contained with its own methods, vocabulary, and concepts.[31]

Poststructuralism has given rise to a number of different schools of thought and methodological procedures. We briefly describe four of them that might be of especial interest to liturgists.

Deconstructionism

Dating to the late 1960s with proponents such as Jacques Derrida (1930–) and Michel Foucault (1926–1984), deconstructionism asserts that we cannot stand completely free of the structures of meaning; any attempt to describe objective structures necessarily implies a position outside and apart from those structures. Every text, then, is incomplete.[32] A text's incompleteness derives precisely from the position that texts have no extra-textual reference. "According to Derrida, the creation and retrieval of meaning ought to be seen as a never ending process in which meanings and systems are always by necessity fluid. 'The absence of the transcendental signified extends the domain and the play of signification indefinitely.'"[33]

Deconstructionism is concerned with the processes that cause sign systems to destabilize and call into question the very meanings they

---

Interpretation of a liturgical text, it seems to me, must always have extra-textual implication.

31. Cf. William A. Beardslee, "Poststructuralist Criticism," in Steven L. McKenzie and Stephen R. Haynes, eds., *To Each Its Own Meaning: An Introduction to Biblical Criticisms and Their Application* (Louisville, Ky.: Westminster/John Knox Press, 1993) 221.

32. Cf. Beardslee, "Poststructuralist Criticism," 221.

33. Jeanrond, *Theological Hermeneutics*, 103, quoting Jacques Derrida, *Writing and Difference*, trans. with intro. and notes by Alan Bass (Chicago: University of Chicago Press, 1978) 280.

produce. It tends to reverse the binary opposites so essential for structuralist schools and deploy them in another direction. The deconstructionist is interested in delivering "the interpreter from the repression of limits and traditions, so that fresh interpretation may take place."[34] On the one hand, "structuralism looks for a determinate deeper structure in the linguistic network"; on the other hand, deconstructionism "emphasizes the openness, the play, of the network of relations, the imperfections in the text that disallow any thoroughly consistent patterns, with the aim of freeing the reader or hearer to make her or his own creative discovery of transient meaning."[35]

It would take us far astray to go into the complexities of deconstructionism with any kind of comprehensiveness or depth. However, another important concept we wish to consider briefly is that Derrida establishes repetition as the condition of possibility for signification and says that the sign must be repeatable in any number of different contexts.[36] This severs the sign from any tie to an empirical or determinable speaker. Ultimately, this strategy undermines the preference of speech over writing.[37] To take this position,

34. Beardslee, "Poststructuralist Criticism," 222. The incompleteness of language or discourse is a great concern of deconstructionists, and especially Derrida. If analysis is closed, there can be no innovation. If textual analysis is allowed to be incomplete, tentative, open-ended, then newness can emerge. I wish to make two points here:

1) Exactly what some interpreters pass over in a text Derrida and other deconstructionists find interesting and challenging: footnotes, glosses, metaphors, turns of language. For example, the content of Derrida's *Margins of Philosophy* (trans. with additional notes by Alan Bass [Chicago: University of Chicago Press, 1982]) is interesting enough in itself; the text is at once both poetic and philosophical. Even more interesting—and to the point here—is that the very layout of the book emphasizes snatches of text, seemingly unimportant in themselves, but Derrida develops them into interesting essays.

2) Because the deconstructionists emphasize the plurality of texts, they also are challenging to existing social order and orthodoxy because they undermine the stability of the systems that keep these ideologies in control. Deconstructionists identify with the marginalized, resisting choice and keeping options open. Derrida's seminal work is *Of Grammatology,* trans. Gayatri Chakravorty Spivak (Baltimore and London: The Johns Hopkins University Press, 1976).

35. Beardslee, "Poststructuralist Criticism," 223.

36. Cf. Derrida, *Writing and Difference,* 281: ". . . there is no transcendental or privileged signified and that the domain or play of signification henceforth has no limit. . . ."

37. Cf. Derrida, *Of Grammatology,* 74–75; also Anthony C. Thiselton, *New*

Derrida transposes the structural task of intra-textual interpretation (a radically synchronic method[38]) to the deconstructive task of *inter*-textual interpretation. "Hence, the differential system of sounds and words studied by de Saussure and structuralist linguistics has now been transposed onto the level of texts."[39] The key here is Derrida's notion of presence. In the speaking situation (or in critical hermeneutical methods that allow for extra-textual vehemence), the presence of the speaker (or author) is crucial to the hermeneutical process. The end of interpretation is to recover this presence.[40] Derrida deconstructs "all those myths of presence in the Western tradition" and emphasizes the "movement of differences" in written language; language is the "real locus of meaning," and so text "emerges from Derrida's thought as a new and fluid entity."[41] A text's semantic autonomy allows for limitless interpretive possibilities and innovation. Derrida offers us an open-ended interpretive approach.

Any interpretive method that denies extra-textual reference always poses problems for liturgical hermeneutics. Among these problems would certainly be listed no ontology, no authority to a text, and no concept of embedded meaning. Deconstructionism, though, has its attractive features for a liturgical hermeneut,[42] namely, its insistence on the possibility of innovation in interpretation and its emphasis on inter-textual relationships. Since liturgy is mystery, it is necessarily open-ended.[43] This suggests that there will always be

---

Horizons in Hermeneutics: The Theory and Practice of Transforming Biblical Reading (Grand Rapids, Mich.: Zondervan, 1992) 104.

38. Derrida is trying to preserve language from the closed meaning of structuralism; cf. Derrida, *Writing and Difference*, 26–29.

39. Jeanrond, *Theological Hermeneutics*, 103.

40. Cf. Derrida, *Writing and Difference*, 279–280 and 292; also *Of Grammatology*, 18–19.

41. Jeanrond, *Theological Hermeneutics*, 103. Derrida is claiming that there is no intersubjectivity, only intertextuality.

42. To my knowledge, other than the extent to which feminist critique has affinities with deconstructionism, no liturgist has attempted any serious deconstruction of a liturgical text.

43. Some writers see value for theological and biblical interpretation because "such a model of textuality" as deconstructionism can deliver us "from bondage to fixed entities and to false securities, and as allowing language to point *towards* the transcendent by polyvalent parable, rather than by having to articulate the transcendent in and through conceptual language" (Thiselton, *New Horizons*, 113).

new and innovative interpretations of that mystery.[44] Also, rather than treat each liturgical text as a discrete entity, deconstruction would have liturgists recognize that innovation with respect to the meaning of the mystery we are trying to interpret may be the result of allowing the liturgical texts to dialogue among themselves. For example, how might the baptismal liturgy shed interpretive light on the Eucharistic liturgy, vis-à-vis the paschal mystery?

Feminist Critique

More an ideology than a methodology, the feminist critique seeks to "expose the culturally based presuppositions embodied in classic discourse."[45] There are almost as many positions on feminism as there are feminists,[46] but there is general agreement that

---

44. New and innovative interpretations are nothing new in liturgy. Compare, for example, the interpretations of the patristics and the scholastics. Or even consider the different (sometimes conflicting) interpretations of a single scriptural event put forth by a patristic writer of the allegorical school. Another case at point: the deconstructionists would denounce the Roman Catholic Church's position on transubstantiation as the only interpretation for what happens to the bread at Eucharist as giving definitive authority to one interpretation.

45. Danna Nolan Fewell, "Reading the Bible Ideologically: Feminist Criticism," in McKenzie and Haynes, *To Each Its Own Meaning,* 239.

46. This not so much because there is disagreement among feminist writers (although there is also that) but because different writers work in different areas. An overview of feminist criticism schools is provided in Elaine Showalter, ed., *The New Feminist Criticism: Essays on Women, Literature, and Theory* (New York: Pantheon, 1985). The literature abounds, but I list here several representative areas and authors; my decision on what to include is based on what I consider varied methodological examples. These works contain bibliographical notes to supplement this short list. I include only works pertinent to the religious domain, simply in the interest of brevity. Feminist writers and works pertaining to liturgy/worship are discussed in chapter 5.

Scripture: Letty Russell, ed., *Feminist Interpretation of the Bible* (Philadelphia: Fortress Press, 1985); Sandra Schneiders, *Women and the Word: The Gender of God in the New Testament and the Spirituality of Women* (New York and Mahwah, N.J.: Paulist Press, 1987); Elisabeth Schüssler Fiorenza, *In Memory of Her: A Feminist Theological Reconstruction of Christian Origins* (New York: Crossroad, 1984) and *But She Said: Feminist Practices of Biblical Interpretation* (Boston: Beacon, 1992); Phyllis Trible, *God and the Rhetoric of Sexuality* (Philadelphia: Fortress Press, 1978) and *Texts of Terror* (Philadelphia: Fortress Press, 1984).

Theology: Anne Carr, *Transforming Grace: Christian Tradition and Women's Experience* (San Francisco: Harper & Row, 1988); Mary Daly, *Gyn-Ecology: The*

texts are "gendered," that is, they do not escape the gender bias of the text producer(s). Feminism shares with structuralism "no pretense to objectivity; it challenges the notion of universals; it is more interested in relevance than in so-called absolute truth."[47] Feminism is in the line of deconstructionism in that it inverts the binary opposite male/female[48] (and others) and sees gender polarity in a new context and looks for innovative meaning in classical texts.[49] Feminism pursues the deconstruction of the myths of an androcentric system and its agenda of power, knowledge, and economics. Alternately, feminism seeks a fluid and creative lifestyle with different expressions of relationships in such areas as family, society, work place, academic arena, and religion.

A feminist critique raises some interesting and significant questions with respect to liturgy. On the positive side (indicating some gains), we might ask, How has the fact of women undertaking visible liturgical ministries affected the actual celebration of liturgy? How has the renewal of liturgy since Vatican II promoted liturgical

Metaphysics of Radical Feminism and the End of Traditional Religions (Boston: Beacon Press, 1978); Sally McFague, *Metaphoric Theology: Models of God in Religious Language* (Philadelphia: Fortress Press, 1982); Elizabeth E. Johnson, *She Who Is: The Mystery of God in Feminist Theological Discourse* (New York: Crossroad, 1993); Rosemary Radford Ruether, *Sexism and God Talk: Toward a Feminist Theology* (Boston: Beacon Press, 1983) and *Women-Church: Theology and Practice* (San Francisco: Harper & Row, 1986); A. B. Ulanov, *Receiving Woman: Studies in the Psychology and Theology of the Feminine* (Philadelphia: The Westminster Press, 1981).

Spirituality: Joann Wolski Conn, *Women's Spirituality: Resources for Christian Development* (New York: Paulist Press, 1986); J. De Vinck, *Revelations of Women Mystics: From Middle Ages to Modern Times* (New York: Alba House, 1985); Francis Eigo, ed., *A Discipleship of Equals: Towards a Christian Feminist Spirituality* (Villanova, Pa.: Villanova University Press, 1988); Monika Hellwig, "The Critical Function of Feminine Spirituality," *Commonweal* 112 (1985) 164–168; Maria Riley, *Wisdom Seeks Her Way: Liberating the Power of Women's Spirituality* (Washington: Center of Concern, 1987).

47. Fewell, "Reading the Bible Ideologically: Feminist Criticism," in McKenzie and Haynes, *To Each Its Own Meaning*, 238.

48. Carol Gilligan, for example, makes much use of binary opposites; see her *In a Different Voice* (Cambridge, Mass.: Harvard University Press, 1982).

49. An important text for biblical exegetes sensitive to feminist criticism is the creation account of humanity in Genesis. For a summary of various approaches to this text and the various positions exegetes take, see Fewell, "Reading the Bible Ideologically: Feminist Criticism," in McKenzie and Haynes, *To Each Its Own Meaning*, 239–247.

innovation disclosing a feminine perspective? Have binary opposites been reversed and recontextualized, giving them new meaning? On the negative side (indicating some areas where seemingly little progress has been made), we might ask, How can an *editio typica*, with multiple translations, even address the many demands of inculturation, let alone the gender issues? Has the gender bias uncovered by feminist critique in both the texts and celebration of liturgy been adequately addressed (or addressed at all)? How do androcentric issues of power and closed systems and closed discussions affect liturgy? Is the Church recognizing the diverse worship of feminist groups and taking sincere steps to understand and accept them?

Narrative Criticism

Dating from the late 1970s and applied to Christian Scriptures more than Hebrew Scriptures, narrative criticism[50] belongs to the text-centered structuralist movement. "Here meaning is to be found by close reading that identifies formal and conventional structures of the narrative, determines plot, develops characterizations, distinguishes point of view, exposes language play, and relates all to some overarching, encapsulating theme."[51] One characteristic of narrative criticism, then, is that it pays attention to the *whole* text (i.e., the entire

50. For a survey of narrative critics dealing with the Hebrew Scriptures, see David M. Gunn, "Narrative Criticism," in McKenzie and Haynes, *To Each Its Own Meaning*, 172–178. For an example of narrative criticism, see Gunn's analysis of the story of Lot at Sodom in Genesis 19, pp. 178–192.

51. Gunn, "Narrative Criticism," in McKenzie and Haynes, *To Each Its Own Meaning*, 171. Robert Scholes and Robert Kellogg, in *The Nature of Narrative* (London, Oxford, and New York: Oxford University Press, 1966) give a simple definition of narrative: "By narrative we mean all those literary works which are distinguished by two characteristics: the presence of a story and a story-teller. . . . For writing to be narrative no more and no less than a teller and a tale are required" (4).

One of the most remarkable texts on narrativity is Paul Ricoeur's *Time and Narrative*, 3 vols., trans. Kathleen McLaughlin and David Pellauer (Chicago and London: University of Chicago Press, 1984, 1985, 1988). For an accessible introductory work, see Mark Allan Powell, *What Is Narrative Criticism?* (Minneapolis, Minn.: Fortress Press, 1990); see also Robert Alter, *The Art of Biblical Narrative* (New York: Basic Books, 1981). For narrativity in the theological domain, see "Genre, Narrativity, and Theology," *Semeia* 43 (1988); see also Hans W. Frei, *Theology and Narrative: Selected Essays*, ed. George Hunsinger and William C. Placher (New York and Oxford: Oxford University Press, 1993).

story). Another characteristic, similar to rhetorical criticism,[52] is that narrative criticism is also interested in the reader. In this case, however, the interest is not in an actual reader of the text but in an idealized "implied" reader "who is presupposed by and constructed from the text itself."[53] As the name implies, narrative criticism is limited to analyzing only narratives. Thus this method is a specific one that cannot be applied to every piece of literature.[54]

Narrative critics would share with semioticians the stance that narratives begin someplace (called the "begin state") and lead the reader someplace else (called the "end state"). That transformation is unfolded in the telling of the story. Different critics may list different narrative elements, but they at least include characters, plot, the point of view from which the story is told (e.g., from the viewpoint of the antagonist or protagonist or a disinterested bystander), setting, and meaning. One of the advantages of narrative criticism is that it underscores the transformative movement in a narrative, in the telling of the story.

This last point has significant ramifications for liturgy. If the purpose of all ritual is transformation, then we might consider liturgy as narrative at two levels. On the one hand, we might analyze the narrative sections of liturgy (for example, in the Eucharistic Prayers) for their transformative movement. To borrow language from semiotics, we might examine the begin state at the Preface and the end state at the great Amen. What moved the assembly from the Preface dialogue to the great Amen? How does the transformation taking place (structurally, if not existentially) in the Eucharistic Prayer relate to the Liturgy of the Word? To the communion rite?

On the other hand, we might analyze an entire rite as a narrative. Here the task of the narrative critic would be to identify the begin state at the opening of the rite and the end state at its conclusion. What is the parallel transformative movement in the assem-

52. See p. 57 above.

53. Powell, *What Is Narrative Criticism?*, 15. Powell asserts that the implied reader's response can be detected from clues in the text (19). He gives the following example: "[T]he implied reader of the Gospels surely knows that a talent is worth more than a denarius (the text assumes this), although real readers today might not have this knowledge" (20).

54. Scholes and Kellogg decry, on the other hand, the fact that narrative literature has been all too narrow in its focus on the novel. Their agenda is to look at the whole panorama of narrative literature—past, present, and even future (see *The Nature of Narrative*, 5–9).

bly? In their subsequent Christian living? Approaching a liturgical text as a narrative gives impetus to perceiving a mimetic relationship between the transformative movement in the liturgical text and transformation in our Christian living.

Reader-response Criticism

Once we put aside the agenda of the critical hermeneuts to recover the authorial intention, history, and context, the way is paved to pay attention to the text *qua* text. But once we put aside the agenda of the purely synchronic school to stay within a text, the way is paved to pay attention to the reader. Essentially, reader-response theory allows for the diachronic and synchronic dimensions of a text to interrelate.

As with many of these post-critical theories and methods, reader-response criticism envelops a number of positions; there is no monolithic approach among its practitioners. What is common, however, is deciphering the role the actual reader plays in the production of a text's meaning. We saw above that narrative criticism is concerned with an idealized, "implied" reader; that is, the reader assumed by (and within) the text itself. With reader-response criticism, we are concerned with the *actual* reader of the text. This interpretive stance, then, breaks with structuralism in that it moves interpretation outside the text. In fact, we might speak of the dialectic or interrelationship of the "horizon of the text" and the "horizon of the reader."[55] Further, what is common among proponents of this approach is "the background of New Criticism, with its insistence on the structural unity of a literary work and the process of close reading that uncovers that structure."[56]

The gamut of relationships of reader to text may be illustrated by the positions taken by Stanley Fish and Wolfgang Iser.[57] The early

55. Cf. Anthony C. Thiselton, "Reader-Response Hermeneutics, Action Models, and the Parables of Jesus," in Roger Lundin, Anthony C. Thiselton, and Clarence Walhout, *The Responsibility of Hermeneutics* (Grand Rapids, Mich.: William B. Eerdmans/Paternoster Press, 1985) 94–95.

56. Edgar V. McKnight, "Reader-Response Criticism," in McKenzie and Haynes, *To Each Its Own Meaning,* 197. The "New Criticism" to which McKnight refers is what we have called "post-critical."

57. For a representative work from the early Fish, see his "Literature in the Reader: Affective Stylistics," in *Self-Consuming Artifacts* (Berkeley and Los Angeles: University of California Press, 1972); for later Fish, see *Is There a Text in This Class? The Authority of Interpretive Communities* (Cambridge: Harvard

Fish came down more on the side of synchronicity: the text has a given meaning and informed readers come to basically the same interpretation of its meaning in the temporal process of reading. The later Fish came down on the diachronic side of the reader: interpretation is wholly a reader process. In order to somewhat mitigate this latter, extreme position of subjectivity, Fish contends that readers are members of interpretive communities; there is a kind of "check and balance" in the reading process to the extent that a reader's interpretation is consistent with the interpretations of other readers in the interpretive community (but allowing for some differences in those interpretations). Iser takes a middle position between early and later Fish: meaning is both given in texts and is the product of text reading. Iser maintains the integrity of a text, but admits that a text is not complete; there are "gaps" in the text that the reader supplies. Thus reader imagination plays a role in the interpretive process. For Iser, interpretation, then, is a dialectic or exchange between text and reader.[58] The reader makes connections between "themes" of subunits in the text at the same time the reader connects the text as a whole. Iser uses the term "negativity"[59] to mean the "development of an overarching idea as the 'basic force' in literary communication"[60] that is to be experienced rather than explained.[61]

University Press, 1980). For a representative work from Iser, see *The Act of Reading: A Theory of Aesthetic Response* (Baltimore and London: Johns Hopkins University Press, 1978).

58. James M. Schmitmeyer puts it this way: ". . . an ancient text carries within it a meaning that is waiting to be released through interaction with contemporary experience. . . . meaning arises more from being embraced by a text than by extracting something from it. In this way, a centuries-old text takes on a new life, shaping and altering the reader's perception and experience of reality" ("Blueprints, Construction Sites, and Homily Preparation," *Liturgical Ministry* 1 [1992] 27).

59. See Iser, *The Act of Reading*, 225–231.

60. McKnight, "Reader-Response Criticism," in McKenzie and Haynes, *To Each Its Own Meaning*, 199. McKnight goes on to explain the perspective from which the term "negativity" makes sense: negativity is the "written base that conditions the formulations of the text by means of the 'gaps'" (199). Iser contends that "negativity is not formulated by the text, but from the unwritten base. . . . It enables the written words to transcend their literal meaning, to assume a multiple referentiality, and so to undergo the expansion necessary to transplant them as a new experience into the mind of the reader" (*The Act of Reading*, 226).

61. Iser, *The Act of Reading*, 226.

In these three relationships of text and reader we again visit our question of the status of the text. In reader-response criticism, the uncompromised synchronic status of the structuralist schools gives way to a combined synchronic/diachronic *process* of interpretation. More than simply a recovery of a given meaning from a text, reader-response theory emphasizes the interaction of reader and text. Because of the role of the actual reader in the process of interpretation (this is to say that the reader's context figures in meaning), reader-response theory also emphasizes the *effect* of reading (interpretation) on the reader. Here we see affinities with rhetorical criticism as well as with Ricoeur's third methodic moment of appropriation.

With its accent on text/reader interrelationship, reader-response criticism has enormous implications for interpretation of liturgical texts. First, it would underscore the *active* role of the whole assembly in liturgical celebration (another way to approach "participation"). The liturgical text has an integrity (truth) of its own at the same time that it interacts with the context of those who are celebrating to produce the meaning of the text in the here-and-now for this assembly.

Second, it would underscore the effect of the text (celebration) on the assembly. Living the meaning of liturgy is a constitutive part of the interpretive process; it relates liturgy and life. Moreover, it suggests that the act of liturgical interpretation is not complete until there has been actual transformation in the subject-reader (the assembly).

Third, it would underscore the role of imagination and aesthetic response during the liturgical act. The assembly can never play a passive role but is always together breaking open the meaning of liturgy (the paschal mystery). The liturgical assembly itself is an interpretive community that necessitates dialogue among the members before, during, and after the intepretive process.

Review

Sometimes post-critical methods are viewed skeptically by serious hermeneuts steeped in the critical methods, especially when some of those methods seem to be little more than word games. Sometimes post-critical hermeneuts scorn the critical methods as placing too much authority in texts and ignore their findings. In fact, our overview[62] of methods in these two chapters alerts us to the

62. Admittedly, the material in these two chapters is brief and incomplete. No attempt has been made to include all the scholars who have proposed

diversity of approaches that derive from the various questions that can be put to a text. In short, no one method can answer all those questions.

Rarely can an interpreter commit herself or himself to a single method and use only that method. Indeed, even in our brief descriptions of methods we see much overlap. For example, in rhetorical criticism we would also be engaging tenets of reader-response criticism. It is clear, too, that a good hermeneut would be somewhat familiar with many methods and have proficiency in more than one. The overlapping of methods also alerts us to the fact that the distinction between the critical and post-critical methods is hardly as sharp as we sometimes think. The questions addressed by the methods might be mutually exclusive but, in fact, all methods still must, at least theoretically, account for author, text, and reader (interpreter).

Different literary genres may benefit from one method as opposed to another. Genre would be one consideration in choice of method. The training and skills of the hermeneut would be another consideration. For example, if one would not know the biblical languages, many of the critical methods would be compromised; if one would not have a fine grasp of linguistic structures, many of the post-critical methods would be compromised. Another criterion for choice of method would be the purpose of the interpretive process. For example, if one is simply reading Sacred Scripture for devotional prayer, method would be less significant than if one is reading Scripture to prepare a homily.

All these methods in one way or another have been used with sacred texts; some were developed specifically for biblical interpretation (for example, reader-response criticism). Each method came to be because the other available methods could not respond to a particular problem or concern with a text. This genetic reflection helps us to be mindful not to dismiss any method too quickly.

One final reflection on liturgy before we move on to the next chapter to examine how these methods have been used by liturgical scholars and helped us in our understanding of liturgy. Liturgy, as a sacred text, has more at stake than, say, literature. That "more at stake" is precisely the recognition of extra-textual reality, namely,

---

different theories and methods. This would take us completely outside the scope of this work. My intention is to make clear the status of author, text, and reader in a range of methods.

the sacred. This does not say that we could not benefit by using methods that are wholly synchronic. It does say that we must have a dialogue of interpretations if we are to understand liturgy as a divine/human encounter.

5 Hermeneutics and Liturgical Studies Today

Compared with the larger development of theology itself, liturgical studies is truly still in its infancy. Dating only to the middle of the nineteenth century, the liturgical movement began primarily out of pastoral concerns. Already by the early decades of the twentieth century, this new movement began to complement pastoral reflection with serious theological reflection, having beginnings at the German Benedictine monastery of Maria Laach with monks such as Dom Odo Casel. Perhaps the crowning moment of the liturgical movement and the most significant impetus officially given to liturgical studies came on 4 December 1963 when the Council Fathers promulgated with a near unanimous vote *Sacrosanctum Concilium*, the Constitution on the Sacred Liturgy. Hardly was the ink dry on this momentous document when it became the bible for a new breed of theologian called "liturgist." Liturgical studies was born in the liturgical movement; it entered its adolescence in those years prior to the Council with the work of the preparatory schema on liturgy.

Theologians, especially those trained in sacramental theology, dove into this inspiring, rapidly developing branch of theology with singular abandon. Summer schools in liturgical studies sprang up and did not want for students. The venerable *Orate Fratres* changed its name to *Worship* and was devoured by theologian, pastor, and student alike. During this flurry of study and research, the *Didache*, Justin's *First Apology*, Hippolytus' *Apostolic Tradition*, and many other texts were dissected minutely for every grain of liturgical wisdom that could be gleaned. Egeria's *Diary of a Pilgrim* became the basic text for entire courses on the fourth-century Jerusalem

Church and its liturgy. Within only about a decade after the Council, all the liturgical rites of the Western Church were revised. A whole new vocabulary became household words: *epiclesis, anamnesis, mystagogy, paschal mystery,* even the word *liturgy* itself. Virtually all these liturgical studies and subsequent publications were historical-critical in methodology. Compendia of extant rites became the textbooks of the liturgical enthusiasts. These texts were studied for their historical contexts and uses. Questions of authorship, theological import, elements of the rite, and literary features were raised.

Rich as these historical-critical studies were (and remain the backbone even today for the serious liturgical scholar), new questions began to emerge that these methods could not address. Already in the early 1970s we find voices that were using different vocabulary and pointing to innovative methods. Today, after three decades of liturgical adaptation, we are faced with the overwhelming, and sometimes discouraging, fact that the desired renewal has not occurred. This does not mean that we have wasted three decades. Quite the contrary: we had to live through our adolescence in order to sharpen the issues and questions that face us. We have learned much. Now we are in a mature position to promote a dialogue of methods and take up their challenges to personal and communal transformation that promises the liturgical renewal we all desire.

The gain in methods allowing literary criticism and biblical studies, anthropology and psychology, philosophy and hermeneutics to take great strides forward has also benefited liturgical studies. We now turn to these new liturgical voices and methods.[1]

---

1. It is not my intention to give a bibliographical accounting of all the new developments in liturgical studies. Instead, I outline major methodological and theoretical vectors in liturgical studies over the past three decades that have capitalized on post-critical methods and theoretical positions. As in previous chapters, I only give one or other citation of a liturgist's work that best illustrates the method or position. Other references to scholars working with post-critical methods can be garnered from the notes and bibliographies in the works cited.

I concentrate my remarks largely on North American liturgists. For a good overview and references on the developments of liturgical method in European scholarship, see the two essays by Renato De Zan, "Criticism and Interpretation of Liturgical Texts" and "Liturgical Textual Criticism" in Anscar J. Chupungco, ed., *Introduction to the Liturgy,* Vol. 1 of *Handbook for Liturgical Studies* (Collegeville, Minn.: The Liturgical Press, 1997) 331–379.

A New Direction for Liturgical Studies

Much of the post-critical work in liturgical studies has been more in the line of borrowing theories and aspects of methods rather than a wholesale, rigorous use of specific methods.[2] Occasional articles and books with hints of this new direction continue to appear.

Liturgical Studies

One of the earliest ventures into a post-critical reflection is an article by French philosopher Jean Ladrière promoting speech-act theory to interpret liturgical language.[3] This is a significant article because it draws attention specifically to the uses of liturgical language. For Ladrière, "The basic problem is to discover how liturgical language works." He says liturgical language is unique in that it is "operative," that is, it "is characterized . . . in a certain form of action; it puts something into practice."[4] Although performativity, since it is concerned with the relationship of a speech-act to interlocutors, might more strictly belong to rhetorical criticism,[5] Ladrière places it in the broader framework of the linguistic analysts, and hence under the post-critical umbrella. Early on in his article he makes the important distinction between syntax, semantics, and pragmatics. His overall concern is to see how the diverse languages in liturgy are really *one* language.[6] Although this article has not spawned any great amount of research on performativity and liturgical language, it remains a groundbreaking piece.[7]

Needless to say, research using critical methods has not been displaced, nor should it be. Much valuable research is still being done using critical methods. Since this research using critical methods has attended liturgical studies from its beginning, they are more familiar and so are omitted here.

2. Some are doing this, however, as we see in the second and third sections of the chapter.

3. Jean Ladrière, "The Performativity of Liturgical Language," trans. John Griffiths, *Concilium* 9/1 (1973) 50–62.

4. Ibid., 51.

5. Which we have listed under the critical methods because of its diachronicity. Other methodologists place all the literary methods in the post-critical camp.

6. Ladrière, "The Performativity of Liturgical Language," 55.

7. Performativity is by no means a dead issue for liturgists. See Wade T. Wheelock, "The Problem of Ritual Language: From Information to Situation," *Journal of the American Academy of Religion* 50 (1982) 49–71; on pp. 52–59 he

Geoffrey Wainwright addresses "The Language of Worship"[8] from a very different perspective. Recognizing the breadth of language use, he puts forth four "angles" from which language might be viewed (theological, historical, social, and aesthetic) and applies them (and numerous subcategories) to worship. Throughout his earlier work *Doxology: The Praise of God in Worship, Doctrine and Life: A Systematic Theology*,[9] he refers to different kinds of language use, for example performativity,[10] "language games,"[11] and he recognizes the limits of language (passim).

Two larger works deserve attention in this general survey of liturgists borrowing from or leaning toward the use in liturgical theology of post-critical methods.

Lawrence A. Hoffman's *Beyond the Text: A Holistic Approach to Liturgy*[12] sensitizes us to a kind of text study that takes seriously the

---

specifically addresses speech acts. See also J. H. Ware, Jr., *Not with Words of Wisdom: Performative Language and Liturgy* (Washington: University Press of America, 1981); and my *Liturgy as Language of Faith: A Liturgical Methodology in the Mode of Paul Ricoeur's Textual Hermeneutics* (Lanham, New York, and London: University Press of America, 1988) 102–103, and the accompanying application to Eucharistic Prayer II. In my article "Homily as Proclamation" (*Liturgical Ministry* 1 [1992] 10–16), I explore proclamation as a unique speech-act in that it is "locutionary, illocutionary, and perlocutionary at one and the same time" (13). For an entirely different approach to proclamation but one that still focuses on language itself (as proclamation and response), see James Empereur, *Exploring the Sacred* (Washington: Pastoral Press, 1987), chap. 9: "Liturgy as Proclamation," 119–132. Gail Ramshaw-Schmidt, in "The Language of Eucharistic Praying" (*Worship* 57 [1983] 419–437), briefly refers to speech-act theory (421–422) in a good overview article on the uses of language in liturgy. For a different approach, see Margaret Mary Kelleher, "Hermeneutics in the Study of Liturgical Performance," *Worship* 67 (1993) 292–318.

8. In Cheslyn Jones, Geoffrey Wainwright, Edward Yarnold, and Paul Bradshaw, eds. *The Study of Liturgy*, rev. ed. (London: SPCK/New York: Oxford University Press, 1992) 519–528. Daniel B. Stevick addresses language *in* worship; see his *Language in Worship: Reflections on a Crisis* (New York: Seabury Press, 1970) and "Language of Prayer," *Worship* 52 (1978) 542–560.

9. New York: Oxford University Press, 1980.

10. For example, p. 18: "In both God and humans, *logos* is performative: it expresses being and engages the person."

11. From the analytic philosophy school, for example, p. 20.

12. Lawrence A. Hoffman, *Beyond the Text: A Holistic Approach to Liturgy* (Bloomington and Indianapolis: Indiana University Press, 1987). For a review-essay of this work, see J. Michael Joncas, "Lawrence A. Hoffman's 'Holistic' Approach to Liturgical Studies," *Questions Liturgiques* 72 (1991) 89–107.

worshipers' engagement with a text (we hear echoes of reader-response theory here),[13] the web of relationships that are part of a worship context (an extension and application of a structuralist concern), and the whole realm of human activity and affectivity that properly belong to the worship act (cutting across rhetorical and other literary concerns). One of the most compelling aspects of Hoffman's work is his eclectic use of different methods. For example, he is comfortable with a penetrating analysis of "geographical" methods to approach rites and marks as an error "the confusion of geographic and social distance";[14] at the same time he is comfortable with a semiotic analysis of the numinous,[15] to name just two methods he uses.

Hoffman's work is much more than a conglomeration of diverse (Jewish) liturgical topics and esoteric methods. He constantly helps us make connections not only between elements within texts but among texts. His is truly a holistic approach to liturgy. Hoffman preserves the worshiping community as the *creating* subject of a ritual. His work is a fine study in methodology: not just of a number of specific post-critical methods but a study of what can be gained by a *dialogue* among those analytic methods. His dialogue of methods makes apparent for liturgists that text as normative ritual and text as created by the celebrating community are both to be taken seriously, neither at the expense of the other.

A second larger work that deserves attention is Kevin W. Irwin's *Context and Text: Method in Liturgical Theology*[16] in which he seeks to relate liturgy and theology by paying close attention to the relationship

13. Although Hoffman pays close attention to text, he comments early on in his book that it "is not the text, then, but the people who pray it, that should concern us" (2). His extra-textual bias (with which I, admittedly, have great affinity, as we will see below in the third section of this chapter) is clearly stated: "Of course research must begin with the literature in which the evidence is embedded; that indeed is necessary. But both philology and form-criticism end with that literature as well; and that is not necessary at all" (5).

14. Hoffman, *Beyond the Text*, 55; this analysis comprises chapter 3, "Rites: A Case of Social Space," 46–59.

15. Hoffman, *Beyond the Text*, chapter 7, "The Numinous: A Problem of Recognition," 149–171, especially pp. 158ff.

16. Kevin W. Irwin, *Context and Text: Method in Liturgical Theology* (Collegeville, Minn.: The Liturgical Press, A Pueblo Book, 1994). The thirty-six-page bibliography at the end of the volume is a good summary of works with methodological import.

of various aspects of liturgy.[17] The subtitle of this volume is misleading; Irwin's is more a theoretical framework than a work in method as such and is groundbreaking in this regard.[18] The titles for the three parts of *Context and Text* lay out Irwin's framework: "Relating Liturgy and Theology," "Context is Text: Theology of Liturgy," and "Text Shapes Context: Liturgical Theology." His chapter 2, "Method," reiterates and clarifies in his new context some of the established debates on liturgical "method" at the same time that he clearly calls for a new method. A new method is needed, he contends, because (1) we have focused too much on the ritual *text* and the contemporary emphasis is on *"liturgy as event,"* and (2) the revised rite is "characterized" by a plethora of "variety and options."[19]

As the title suggests, Irwin is arguing that liturgical theology today must be based on text (data) and context (use). Without naming it as such, Irwin is calling for a liturgical theology based on a dialogue of text-based methods and reader- (assembly-) based methods. For example, in chapter 3 on the Word, he comments that "strictly speaking a Liturgy of the Word is never repeated." He goes on to say this is so because "the interaction of this assembly here and now in their personal and communal histories with these texts interacting with each other in ever new and different ways is always new."[20] Irwin identifies for us a new agenda in liturgical interpretation that has been steadily gaining ascendancy: "In accord with the dialectical thesis of this book, two things matter. That the *text* of the liturgy be interpreted in relation to the *context* of our communal and personal lives and that the *context* of all of life be lived in harmony with the *text* of enacted liturgy . . . ."[21]

17. For example, text, context, symbols, ritual gestures.

18. We consider theoretical frameworks in the third section below but include a discussion of Irwin here because his objective was not theoretical but oriented toward liturgical theology. Admittedly, "method" is an equivocal term. I restrict it in this essay to refer to analytic approaches to texts.

19. Irwin, *Context and Text*, 52–53.

20. Ibid., 97.

21. Ibid., 346. In fact, this is hardly a new theme for Irwin, but it has been methodologically sharpened and more systematically presented in *Context and Text*; see his *Liturgy, Prayer and Spirituality* (New York/Ramsey, N.J.: Paulist Press, 1984).

Sacramental Theology

Sacraments are defined in various ways, but essentially the definitions all somehow take in signifier and signified, which intuitively opens the door for a hermeneutical discussion. So it is not surprising that sacramental theology is an area raising hermeneutical questions that theologians and liturgists alike address. As Stephen Happel remarks, "Taking notice of the politics of language is only the most recent part of the linguistic turn in relation to the theology of the sacraments."[22]

An early attempt to redescribe the sacraments in linguistic terms and deal with the perceived inadequacies of our traditional sacramental formulations for today's world is George S. Worgul's *From Magic to Metaphor: A Validation of Christian Sacraments.*[23] According to Worgul, both "external and internal factors" contribute to our current sacramental demise. External factors involve the fact that "human history has entered a new cultural age with new and different presuppositions about the meaning, purpose, and style of life."[24] Internally, Worgul contends that as we have theologically and pastorally accommodated ourselves to the cultural shifts, we have necessarily had to dismantle "the former synthesis," and the rebuilding has required time, resulting in "the feeling of confusion and chaos."[25] Worgul proposes a method that capitalizes on an integrating vision that is at once existential[26] and anthropological.[27] To this end he

22. Stephen Happel, "Worship as a Grammar of Social Transformation, in *The Linguistic Turn and Contemporary Theology: Essays on the Theme,* ed. George Kilcourse, intro. Michael J. Scanlon, Current Issues in Theology 2 (The Catholic Theological Society of America, 1987) 60. This is a significant article for several reasons. First, Happel gives a very fine overview of the use of language theory in new sacramental theologizing (initially dividing his remarks into four "camps": linguistic analysis [including speech-act theory], literary criticism, empirical analyses of social sciences, and phenomenology of language [62ff.]). Second, his notes provide ample bibliographical references, supplying the reader with a good overview of what had been published to 1987. Third, Happel's is a *critical* piece, penetrating the strengths and weaknesses of the various arguments and positions.

23. George S. Worgul, *From Magic to Metaphor: A Validation of Christian Sacraments,* foreword by Piet Fransen (New York/Ramsey, N.J.: Paulist Press, 1980).

24. Ibid., 3.

25. Ibid.

26. He draws on Blondel and Tracy.

27. Worgul, *From Magic to Metaphor,* 33.

draws on a number of post-critical methods and theories[28] and applies his reflections in Part 3 of the book to a redescription of sacramental theology. Perhaps Worgul lacks the methodological precision of later authors and has not gained the reputation among sacramental theologians and liturgists that some others we discuss have. This work does point to a rather early publication that reminds us that new issues and post-critical responses have been on the minds of sacramental theologians and liturgists already for several decades.

Probably the first influential work that pushed sacramental theologians and liturgists in the direction of post-critical methods is David N. Power's *Unsearchable Riches: The Symbolic Nature of Liturgy*.[29] His focus is on symbol,[30] but much more: ritual, verbal image, myth, narrative, metaphor. The title of chapter 6 summarizes most effectively

28. For example, speech-act theory (pp. 71–72), structuralism/functionalism (pp. 94–95), semiotics (pp. 97–98), anthropological models (pp. 98–104).

29. David N. Power, *Unsearchable Riches: The Symbolic Nature of Liturgy* (New York: Pueblo Publishing Company, 1984). No doubt, Power's influence has been due not only to the vigor of his thinking but also to the number of students he has taught and inspired and colleagues with whom he has had dialogues. He remarks on his gratitude for these relationships in the closing paragraph of the preface to *Unsearchable Riches*. But the more telling testimony is the Festschrift in honor of his sixtieth birthday, *A Promise of Presence*, edited by two of his former students, Michael Downey and Richard Fragomeni (Washington: Pastoral Press, 1992). The chapter topics witness to Power's breadth of research as well as his continuing post-critical interests: anthropology, liberation, memory, metaphor, ecumenism, inculturation, language, and event.

For a brief summary (but from a different perspective from my own here) of *Unsearchable Riches* and a critique of Power's use of Ricoeur, see Happel, "Worship as a Grammar of Social Transformation," 76–82. I come back to this critique in the third section of this chapter.

30. It is not surprising that sacramental theologians would grasp on to post-critical methods and directions, given the symbolic foundation of sacraments. In recent decades an abundance of new material on symbol has appeared. Already in 1970 Ernest Skublics explored the psychological dimensions of symbol and liturgy in "Psychologically Living Symbolism and Liturgy" (*Église et Théologie* 1 [1970] 205–228); for an even earlier publication, see David Cox, "Psychology and Symbolism," in *Myth and Symbol*, ed. F. W. Dillistone (London: SPCK, 1966) 51–66. Don E. Saliers, in *Worship as Theology: Foretaste of Glory Divine* (Nashville: Abingdon Press, 1994) has two chapters in this recent contribution to liturgical theology that deal with the symbolic languages of liturgy from different perspectives: chapter 9, "Beyond the Text: The Symbolic Languages of Liturgy," and chapter 10, "The Liturgical 'Canon' in Context."

Power's interest in "The Language and Work of Faith." The question is "whether reflection on the symbolic structure and language of liturgy allows some insight into the manner in which it is both the act of God which sanctifies and the act of the church which gives God glory."[31] Power notes the array of approaches to symbol ("in theology, philosophy, poetics, sociology, anthropology, psychology, or the history of religions")[32] and draws on a number of theorists from different fields to discuss symbol.[33] The "general overview of the nature and functioning of symbol"[34] comprising chapter 3 underscores a "clash of viewpoints"[35] with respect to symbol reflecting the same clash of viewpoints in the development of hermeneutics, that is, the ontological status of symbol or language. Thus early on the central question of hermeneutics is linked to sacramental theology and liturgy.

If Power's is the most influential work in the direction of post-critical methods, Louis-Marie Chauvet's has been the most comprehensive and systematic work published to date with primarily a post-critical approach to sacramental theology.[36] This extraordinary contribution to sacramental theology differs from the previous works we have discussed in that Chauvet works out of a consistent and comprehensive post-critical theoretical framework.[37] The status of the text (and sacramental symbol) is clearly one of *disclosure*, and this shift "will require such a radical overturn of the classical approach"

31. Power, *Unsearchable Riches*, 144.

32. Ibid., 61.

33. For example, psychologist Antoine Vergote, philosophers Paul Ricoeur and Susanne Langer, cultural anthropologist Clifford Geertz, social ethicist Gibson Winter, theologians Louis-Marie Chauvet, Langdon Gilkey, Rudolf Otto, Raimondo Panikkar, David Tracy, etc.

34. Power, *Unsearchable Riches*, 79.

35. Ibid., 78.

36. Louis-Marie Chauvet, *Symbol and Sacrament: A Sacramental Reinterpretation of Christian Existence,* trans. Patrick Madigan and Madeleine Beaumont (Collegeville, Minn.: The Liturgical Press, A Pueblo Book, 1995); published in French in 1987.

37. A very fine methodological exercise that would reveal the radical shift in theoretical and methodological framework gradually introduced over the past decades would be to do a close comparative reading of Chauvet's work with that of Cyprian Vagaggini (*Theological Dimensions of the Liturgy: A General Treatise on the Theology of the Liturgy,* trans. Leonard J. Doyle and W. A. Jurgens [Collegeville, Minn.: The Liturgical Press, 1976]). Especially pay close attention to their very different approaches to symbol.

to sacramentality; on the one hand, "we recognize something of what the Scholastic theory of sacraments attempted to capture with the categories of 'sign' and 'cause'"; on the other hand, "our language is different. Furthermore, this change of language is not merely cosmetic, but constitutes *a fundamental revision of the terms with which we approach the problem:* those of language and symbol, and no longer those of cause and instrument."[38]

Ultimately, Chauvet's agenda is to show that "the sacramental celebrations place us in both the figurative order and the pragmatic order: whatever we are permitted to *see* there is given to us precisely that we may simultaneously *live* it."[39] By changing the "language game,"[40] Chauvet is able to shift from a subject/object relationship (God/grace, with sacraments as mediating entities) to "allowing oneself to be spoken";[41] that is, the language of faith and liturgy is "self-implicative."[42] Chauvet's shift in language, and his emphasis on ontological vehemence in language, enables him to shift the focus of sacramental reality to the celebrating assembly (echoes of reader-response theory) and its appropriation of the liturgical *act* for daily Christian living.

One final sacramental work to which we turn is Peter E. Fink's *Praying the Sacraments.*[43] In chapter 3, "Three Languages of Christian Sacraments," Fink remarks that "liturgy speaks, and it is important both reflectively and pastorally to attend to the ways of its speaking."[44] Shaped by his overall agenda to uncover the *praying* aspects of the sacramental act, Fink identifies three languages of the sacraments: (1) the reflective language of theology, (2) the "evocative and inviting" language of prayer, and (3) the language of "space, of movement, of interaction" that is "the event prior to and independent" of the word.[45] Fink's point is that sacramental celebrations

38. Chauvet, *Symbol and Sacrament,* 2; italics in original; cf. pp. 444–446.

39. Ibid., 2; italics in original.

40. Ibid., 426.

41. Ibid., 446.

42. Ibid., 426–427. Compare Chauvet's "self-implicative" with Donald D. Evans's "self-involvement" (*The Logic of Self-involvement: A Philosophical Study of Everyday Language with Special Reference to the Christian Use of Language About God as Creator* [New York: Herder and Herder, 1969; originally, London: SCM Press, 1963]).

43. Peter E. Fink, *Praying the Sacraments* (Washington: Pastoral Press, 1991).

44. Ibid., 29.

45. Ibid., 30.

must disclose in ritual act what the language says we are doing. For example, if Eucharist is understood to be a shared meal, then the ritual action must indicate that that is exactly what we are doing: sharing a meal. Paying attention to the language of our sacraments opens new dimensions for praying and living the spirituality of the sacraments (and our own personal prayer and spirituality).

Inclusive Language

Works abound on inclusive language; we consider here only those pertinent to our discussion of post-critical methods and liturgy.

Gail Ramshaw couches both her discussion of inclusive language as well as the broader issue of liturgical language use within a framework of metaphor.[46] She draws upon Paul Ricoeur's theory of metaphor to suggest that metaphor is "the distinctive characteristic of the working human mind."[47] It is a (linguistic) tension-producing "use of speech in which the context demonstrates that a factually or logically inaccurate word is on the deepest level true."[48] The classic (and problematic for some) liturgical example is calling God "father." Approached as metaphor, this says that at the factual or literal level, God is not father (biologically understood); at a deeper level, something about the notion of fatherhood can be said about God, and so therefore the statement is true at this deeper level.[49]

Critical reflection on the inclusive language question suggests that several problems are at hand in the issue, and they are not equally easy to address in practical liturgical implementation.[50] I identify three roots of exclusive language.

46. See her *Liturgical Language: Keeping It Metaphoric, Making It Inclusive*, American Essays in Liturgy (Collegeville, Minn.: The Liturgical Press, 1996); also *Searching for Language* (Washington: Pastoral Press, 1988) and *Christ in Sacred Speech: The Meaning of Liturgical Language* (Philadelphia: Fortress Press, 1986). Ramshaw illustrates her points in these texts by analyzing various liturgical texts.

47. Ramshaw, *Liturgical Language*, 9.

48. Ibid., 7.

49. See Power, *Unsearchable Riches*, 158–164, for a similar discussion. Power discusses not only the problem of "father" as a metaphor but also the existential problem of some individuals' negative experiences with their own fathers and how that enters into receiving the metaphor or not.

50. See my article "A Language of Spirituality," *Église et Théologie* 20 (1989) 283–304.

1) Translation of Scripture and other texts that were produced in a language and culture different from our own. The challenge here is twofold: (a) *faithful* translation of the text and (b) reflection of current language usage.[51]

2) Texts that have been produced in an androcentric context and so contain clear androcentric attitudes and positions. The challenge here is to reject "a fundamentalist-literalist, oppressive interpretation" and gain "an insight into the progressive disclosure of the meaning of God's Word for all people of all times."[52]

3) Use of metaphor. The challenge here is to understand the linguistic function of metaphor.[53] Sorting out the different levels of the problem is helpful in itself. Additionally, what cuts across all three levels of the problem (and other areas of the problem not addressed here) is that we are essentially dealing with a linguistic and hermeneutical problem, and it must be addressed as such.

51. See, for example, Lawrence Boadt, "Problems in the Translation of Scripture as Illustrated by ICEL's Project on the Liturgical Psalter," in Peter C. Finn and James M. Schellman, eds., *Shaping English Liturgy* (Washington: Pastoral Press, 1990) 405–429, especially pp. 425–426 on inclusive language.

52. Zimmerman, "A Language of Spirituality," 285. Any number of feminist writings address this issue of androcentric texts and contexts.

53. Ricoeur has written extensively on metaphor. See his "Metaphor and the Central Problem of Hermeneutics," in Paul Ricoeur, *Hermeneutics and the Human Sciences,* ed. and trans. John B. Thompson (Cambridge: Cambridge University Press, 1982) 165–181; also *The Rule of Metaphor: Multi-disciplinary Studies of the Creation of Meaning in Language,* trans. Robert Czerny with Kathleen McLaughlin and John Costello (Toronto, Buffalo, and London: University of Toronto Press, 1977) passim. Especially pertinent is Ricoeur's "Fatherhood: From Phantasm to Symbol," trans. Robert Sweeney, in *The Conflict of Interpretations: Essays in Hermeneutics,* ed. Don Ihde (Evanston, Ill.: Northwestern University Press, 1974) 468–497.

For a more historical methodological approach to naming God, see Mary Collins, *Renewal to Practice* (Washington: Pastoral Press, 1987), chapter 12, "Naming God in Public Prayer," 215–229. The breadth of Collins's scholarship is evident in that she is equally comfortable with post-critical approaches; see her entry "Language, Liturgical," in Peter E. Fink, ed., *The New Dictionary of Sacramental Worship* (Collegeville, Minn.: The Liturgical Press, A Michael Glazier Book, 1990) 651–661, especially pp. 654–661 on "Liturgical Language: Emerging Theoretical Considerations."

Inculturation

Early on, Mary Collins recognized the relationship between methodology and the inculturation question.[54] Countless scholars have remarked on the cultural context of liturgy, especially citing Clifford Geertz's landmark book *The Interpretation of Cultures*.[55] The established "recognized name" in the area of liturgy and culture is Anscar Chupungco.[56] Others, too, have recognized the importance of this area. David Power makes numerous references to the importance of the cultural context for interpretation in his *Unsearchable Riches*, and then he devoted an entire volume to culture and its ramifications for liturgy.[57] Mark Francis is addressing the question from within a North American multicultural context.[58] Attention is being drawn to Hispanic and African American contexts for liturgy; the bibliography is growing larger day by day.[59]

All work on inculturation shares common characteristics: (1) there is a sense of urgency about the work, since today we are keenly aware that liturgy is never celebrated in a context-free environment; (2) there is clear borrowing from the work of social science theorists, who have a longer history of working in this area; (3) there is a keen awareness among sacramental theologians and liturgists working in this area of the theoretical underpinnings of their work, borrowed though they may be. Perhaps the most significant common characteristic is a hint of both urgency and frustration with respect to method. A simple perusal of the *Proceedings of the North American Academy of Liturgy* over the past decade—paying special

54. See her "Liturgical Methodology and the Cultural Evolution of Worship in the United States," *Worship* 49 (1975) 85–102.

55. Clifford Geertz, *The Interpretation of Cultures* (New York: Basic Books, 1973).

56. See his *Cultural Adaptation of the Liturgy* (New York/Ramsey, N.J.: Paulist Press, 1982) and his more recent *Liturgical Inculturation: Sacramentals, Religiosity, and Catechesis* (Collegeville, Minn.: The Liturgical Press, 1992).

57. David N. Power, *Culture and Theology* (Washington: Pastoral Press, 1990).

58. See his *Liturgy in a Multicultural Community*, American Essays in Liturgy (Collegeville, Minn.: The Liturgical Press, 1991). Contains a brief but helpful annotated bibliography.

59. In addition to Mark Francis's work cited above, see Melva Wilson Costen, *American Christian Worship* (Nashville: Abingdon Press, 1993), which is more a historical approach than a post-critical one, but it does point to a growing concern.

attention to the work of the Ritual-Language-Action: Social Sciences Study Group, but not neglecting the work of those working in feminist liturgies and even the Music Study Group—indicates an ever growing need for methodological tools (and they necessarily will be diverse) to interpret more adequately the data. Rather than a weakness, this methodological deficiency points to the relative newness of cultural and contextual concerns and sensitivities. Theory always comes before sound methodology. It points to a fast-growing and much needed research area for liturgical theology.

The methodological challenge in the area of liturgical culture and context is not so simple as borrowing from the more established human sciences with their array of methodologies. We can certainly learn from this work and even analogously apply the methodologies. The difference, however, is that the liturgical question of culture and context has other things at stake that cannot be ignored when searching for method: tradition, permanence of a shared "text" that cuts across cultural boundaries, language (as code and as metalanguage), and the status of sacred texts, to name a few. But most importantly what is at stake is the *reception* of the liturgical text by a worshiping community. Liturgical texts remain not *outside* the worshipers but implicate them at the very level of living (which is also where culture works). The intersection of liturgy and culture is inevitable. It has taken the Western Church over a millennium to rediscover this truth. We can hardly expect to solve the issues overnight. The good news is that the challenge is being taken up seriously by liturgists today.

Post-critical Methods and Liturgical Studies

Many liturgists draw on various post-critical methods to do liturgical interpretation, as we see in the previous remarks. However, we have yet to come into our own in terms of any kind of systematic, sustained use of post-critical methods. We are still enamored with the newness of the enterprise and the breadth of possibilities. A few liturgists are already working consistently with a specific method. Perhaps because it is so clear, well-defined, and easily lends itself to various kinds of textual analysis, the one method that stands out is semiotics. We consider three very different areas of application.

The late liturgist Mark Searle spent sabbatical time in 1989 at Tilburg and participated in the work of the Dutch group SEMANET, composed of biblical exegetes, liturgists, catechists, and philosophers. Their work has been largely concerned with a semiotics of architecture. In the paper distributed to members of the NAAL Ritual-Language-Action: Social Sciences Study Group for discussion at the 1990 meeting, Searle introduced the group to the nature and function of semiotics, then concluded his discussion with analyses of the marriage rite, the blessing of water, and of the parish church of Sts. Peter and Paul in Tilburg, Holland. This last analysis was an especially important one because it alerts us to the fact that "text" is not limited to written texts; church buildings—sacred spaces—are texts as well, and the rules of interpretation can be applied to them.[60]

J. Michael Joncas is well-known as a composer of liturgical music; perhaps he is less well known as a semiotician. Joncas has applied semiotic method to music. In his article "Semiotics and the Analysis of Liturgical Music,"[61] Joncas mentions the possibility that semiotics can "be applied to other codes employed in worship (e.g., kinetic, gestural, postural, olfactory, architectural, color, artifact, textual, personnel) and how they interact."[62] In this article he limits himself to an overview of semiotics, discusses the concepts in relation to music, and discusses the possibilities for analyzing liturgical music. He outlines three advantages. (1) Semiotics might help to clarify various liturgical music forms. (2) Semiotics may help us

---

60. Searle's untimely death prevented him from publishing very much of this work. But for some of his semiotic work, see "Fons Vitae: A Case Study in the Use of Liturgy as a Theological Source [Blessing of Baptismal Water at Easter Vigil]," in *Fountain of Life*, ed. Gerard Austin (Washington: Pastoral Press, 1991) 217–242, and, with Gerard Lukken, *Semiotics and Church Architecture* (Kampen: Kok Pharos, 1993). For a different methodological approach to analyzing sacred space, cf. Richard S. Vosko's "Toward a Systematic Methodology for the Evaluation of Worship Environments," in *Proceedings of the North American Academy of Liturgy*, Annual Meeting Boston, 5–8 January 1995 (Valparaiso, Ind.: NAAL, 1995) 105–113. Also Rainer Volp, "Space as Text: The Problem of Hermeneutics in Church Architecture," *Studia Liturgica* 24 (1994) 168–177.

61. *Liturgical Ministry* 3 (Fall, 1994) 144–154. See also his "Liturgical Musicology and Musical Semiotics: Theoretical Foundations and Analytic Techniques," *Ecclesia Orans* 8 (1991) 181–206, and chapter 14, "Liturgical Music as Music: The Contribution of the Human Sciences," in Robin A. Leaver and Joyce Ann Zimmerman, eds., *Liturgy and Music: Lifetime Learning* (Collegeville, Minn.: The Liturgical Press, 1998).

62. Joncas, "Semiotics and the Analysis of Liturgical Music," 144.

determine how new compositions "emulate" in some organic way the tradition of liturgical music and may function as an adequate medium in today's cultures. (3) Semiotics may help us make sound judgments concerning multicultural music.[63] Joncas is also quite aware of the limitations of semiotics, no small one being the esoteric vocabulary and complex analyses involved. With these cautions in mind, now what is needed is to capitalize on the gains and actually begin to analyze semiotically liturgical music pieces.

Another area where semiotics has already proven helpful is homiletics. John Allyn Melloh has done some work in this area. Like Joncas, he is aware of both the difficulties and benefits of semiotic analysis.[64] In his article "Homily Preparation: A Structural Approach," after listing some basic principles for structural exegesis and identifying what he calls "homily," Melloh offers a clear, three-part, step-by-step method for preparing a homily.[65] Melloh has taken what is an admittedly complex method and translated it so as to be used by someone not fully versed in all the complexities of semiotics.[66]

Semiotics holds much promise as a method for analyzing liturgical texts for those who are willing to wade through the esoteric vocabulary and take time to become familiar with the various analyses. Further, since it is an objective method that examines the relationship of signs within a system, it is able to be applied to many kinds of liturgical texts that have escaped serious analysis to date. The same grammar for uncovering the relationship of signs within a system can also be used to uncover the relationship among sign systems. This holds much promise in that semiotics, as a synchronic method, could enter into a very fruitful dialogue with the traditional diachronic methods liturgists have used to date with such great success. For example, Edward Foley has offered a historical overview of the purpose of liturgical vessels;[67] this work could be nicely complemented by a semiotic analysis of the actual celebrative uses of sacred vessels.

63. Ibid., 154.

64. See his "Homily Preparation: A Structural Approach," *Liturgical Ministry* 1 (1992) 21–26. Although he is calling his approach "structural," he draws on some semiotics approaches (e.g., binary opposites).

65. Ibid., 23–26.

66. For another view of homiletics with post-critical method, see David. G. Buttrick, "On Doing Homiletics Today," in *Intersections: Post-critical Studies in Preaching*, ed. Richard L. Eslinger (Grand Rapids, Mich.: Wm. B. Eerdmans, 1994) 88–104.

67. See his "For a Holy Purpose: Sacrality and Liturgical Vessels," in *Pro-*

Language Issues and Philosophical Framework

Much more work still needs to be undertaken using post-critical methods vis-à-vis liturgical texts. As already mentioned, the tendency has been to outline theories or cull from a theory those elements that show particular promise for liturgical hermeneutics. We said in the previous section of this chapter that it is time now for liturgists to take up specific methods and apply them in their integrity and richness to appropriate liturgical texts.

The same can be said about theory. To date we have referred to many linguistic and hermeneutical theorists who show promise in giving us help for interpreting liturgical texts and addressing the questions that are pertinent today that the traditional critical theories cannot answer. Yet, comprehensive works by liturgists on language issues and hermeneutical theory are still all too scarce. We have tended to be rather eclectic in our approach, drawing on whatever is available to help us address an issue. This is an important strategy when a new field of inquiry is just opening up. But as our survey in this chapter has shown, liturgists have been serious about post-critical methods for three decades now. As we begin to come into our own in terms of the linguistic and philosophical issues involved, we can expect more work of a systematic and integrating nature.

For over a decade now I have been consistently working with Paul Ricoeur's philosophical hermeneutics and believe that I have made available the most complete philosophical framework for a viable liturgical hermeneutics that can capitalize on both critical and post-critical methods. Drawing heavily on his textual hermeneutics, I have also profited hermeneutically from his works on symbolism, metaphor, narrative, imagination, action theory, and return to the subject, to name a few.[68] In each case, nevertheless, I have always been careful to place the particular aspect of his theory with which I might be working within his larger philosophical framework. When some scholars who use only aspects of a theory neglect this larger enterprise, they tend to lay themselves open to warranted criticism.

Some of the problems we encounter when working with Paul Ricoeur are that, as previously mentioned, he has tended not to

---

ceedings of the North American Academy of Liturgy, Annual Meeting, Minneapolis, 2–5 January 1991 (Valparaiso, Ind.: NAAL, 1991) 72–81.

68. My publications drawing on this material have already been cited, so it is not necessary to repeat them here.

publish systematic works on any specific topic or theme.[69] He continually takes his philosophical hermeneutics into new directions,[70] and his published works tend to be very dense. To be at least somewhat competent in Ricoeur means that we must have a broad grasp of a large philosophical enterprise.[71] Moreover, any critique of those borrowing from Ricoeur (or any other theorist, for that matter) would necessarily need to include how the borrowing has been limited by omitting the larger framework.[72] For example, Stephen Happel takes David Power to task for limiting the ontology of sacraments to the referential function of metaphor. He remarks that he believes Power himself understands the limits when he includes the work of Rahner and Schillebeeckx. This may be so. But both are remiss in that they fail to point to the ontological vehemence of Ricoeur's dialectics, especially that of explanation-understanding.

The mistake lies not with Ricoeur. The key here is to understand that Ricoeur preserves an (indirect) ontological vehemence for texts. At the same time, by claiming an ontological thrust for hermeneutics, he is saying nothing (nor are we) about a correspondence between text and an objective reality "out there." Interpretation is

69. Which means that someone cannot read just a little bit of Ricoeur and proceed immediately to apply him to some liturgical area. We need to read much and always integrate that into his larger philosophical framework. Otherwise we tend to distort Ricoeur and use him out of context.

70. In doing so, he always integrates his new direction with his previous work. For this reason, one cannot jump into the middle of Ricoeur but must journey with him from the beginning of his philosophical endeavors.

71. In her response to Stephen Happel's "Worship as a Grammar of Social Transformation," Susan A. Ross comments (indirectly) that perhaps sacramental theologians such as David Power have placed too much credence in Ricoeur and his theories. I would argue that we have tended to use too little of Ricoeur, which has led to some distortions. For example, Ross (rightly) objects to Ricoeur's metaphor as a model for sacramental theology (see her "A Response to Stephen Happel, in *The Linguistic Turn and Contemporary Theology*, 88). The real problem here is not that Ricoeur's notion of metaphor cannot open some doors for a deeper understanding of sacraments and liturgy; I do believe it can. Rather, the real problem is that metaphor cannot be the limit of how we might borrow from Ricoeur for a sacramental theology. His notion of metaphor must always be brought into his larger philosophical framework. In this case, it would be paramount to bring remarks on metaphor into his tripartite dialectical method of participation (pre-understanding)-distanciation (explanation)-appropriation (new self-understanding).

72. See chapter 4, note 14, for my remarks on omitting any mention of dialectics in working with Ricoeur.

primarily an active involvement on the part of the hermeneut—the "reader" of the text—with the text. For Ricoeur, there is always a return to the subject. Ricoeur's methodic hermeneutics may be something of a bridge between the text of liturgy and its actual celebration (as a text in its own right). What this says is that these fledgling methods are making apparent for liturgists the fact that text as normative and text as celebrating community are both to be taken seriously, neither at the expense of the other.

Hopefully, this chapter has opened up new areas for doing liturgical studies. At the same time, we have introduced some cautions. Rather than daunt us, this should awaken us to continue to grasp a direction that only promises new and exciting possibilities.

Epilogue

Method is hardly one of the most scintillating topics for liturgical studies. Many of us readily recall the hours we spent diagraming sentences when we were elementary school students and probably wondered, "What's the use of all this?" Little did we realize that such exercises were sharpening our analytic prowess and giving us insight into the workings of language. Language is one of those things we use all the time—every day in our thought, speech, communication. Few of us pay very much attention at all to the questions, How does it work? Why does it work? When does it work?

That liturgy uses language can hardly be disputed. We do need to sharpen our understanding about exactly what is liturgical language. For too long in the Western Church liturgical language has meant only the verbal. Still, the beauty of the French baroque cathedral or one of Palestrina's polyphonic pieces functioned as language. It all contributed to our holistic experience of liturgy. Today we are in a position to recognize the many languages that comprise a liturgical celebration. With this recognition comes the need to interpret those languages. Since the languages are varied, we might expect, then, that any one interpretation or heuristic method is simply inadequate to deliver for us the richness of what liturgy promises.

"Method" continues to be used equivocally by sacramental theologians and liturgists to mean theory, actual interpretive methods, or even ways of doing liturgy. Perhaps this essay contributes to sharpening our use of the term and opening new avenues for study. One thing is for sure: Since all communication is language and all language begs interpretation—which always includes a surplus of meaning—there can be no such thing as a definitive orthodoxy or orthopraxy. To pursue such is to pursue the wind. The different interpretive methods that have been opening up to liturgists do provide potential for a dialogue of methods that can only draw us deeper into the mystery that we seek to understand. And to be drawn deeper into the mystery is to be inevitably drawn deeper into the Author of that mystery. This makes whatever growing pains we might feel as liturgical methods evolve into their own more than worth both the risks and difficulties.

This essay has tried to show the breadth of the hermeneutic enterprise, both in its inception and use outside the liturgical domain and within the liturgical domain itself. Nonetheless, the reader would be sadly disillusioned if she or he considers this work anything but one that raises questions. Hermeneutics is always open-ended. And so we close with some questions that liturgy and hermeneutics still must take up, even if they will never be satisfactorily answered until we all stand together at the messianic banquet.

- Does the language of liturgy constitute a unique language transcendent in itself?
- Is there a unique "liturgical genre" that constitutes a liturgical text as liturgy?
- What hermeneutical frameworks can best capture the formal and informal aspects of the interpretation of liturgy?
- What method can best deliver for us an ontology? Is this possible? What is at stake in the question of ontology and liturgy?
- Who is the subject of liturgy who interprets its meaning?
- How can we best enter into a dialogue of methods? How do methods complement one another theoretically? Pastorally?
- What are the limits of methods for liturgical texts? What do methods open up?

We began our tour of liturgy and hermeneutics with the many facets of the god Hermes; we end with questions that point to the many facets of liturgy. The contrast between stability and dynamism clearly marks liturgy. Rather than daunt us, liturgy and hermeneutics may excite us to new possibilities for encountering the Sacred in mystery. That is what liturgical celebration is ultimately all about. And so are we.

Index

Jakobson, Roman, 63
Joncas, J. Michael, 86, 97, 98

Kant, Immanuel, 30
Kellogg, Robert, 75, 76

Ladrière, Jean, 85
language, 5, 6, 15–19, 27–29, 32–34,
    37, 38, 40–44, 51, 52, 56, 58,
    62–66, 68, 69, 71, 72, 74–76, 85,
    86, 89–94, 96, 97, 99, 103, 104
    relationship to being, 43
language games, 86
langue, 63
life philosophy, 30
linguistic sign, 62
    for de Saussure, 62
linguistic turn, 62, 89, 100
literary criticism, 24, 30, 56, 57, 64,
    84, 89
liturgical movement, 8, 83
liturgical studies, 6, 8, 23, 29, 39, 48,
    59, 63, 66, 83–86, 96, 101, 103
liturgy, 6–9, 11–21, 23, 26, 37, 39,
    42–46, 48, 49, 51–61, 63–69,
    72–76, 79–81, 83–88, 90–97,
    99–101, 103, 104
    as text, ritual, life, 18
    def., 7, 9
    goal of, 12

meaning, 6, 7, 15–21, 24, 25, 27, 29,
    31–35, 37, 38, 40, 43, 45–50, 52,
    53, 55, 57, 58, 62–79, 93, 94, 104
    as dialectic of sense and
        reference, 18, 20
    def., 17, 20
    def., Ricoeur, 45
    def., de Saussure, 62
    for semiotics, 69
    literal, 6, 27, 93
    residue, 17, 19
    and structure, 45
Melloh, John Allyn, 98

metaphor, 40, 45, 68, 89, 90, 93, 94,
    99, 100
methods, 7, 8, 17, 19, 20, 28, 30, 36,
    38, 39, 44, 47–51, 53–56, 58–64,
    66, 68, 70, 72, 77, 79–81, 84–88,
    90, 91, 93, 96, 98, 99, 101, 103, 104
    critical, 49
    diachronic, 50, 55, 57, 77–79, 98
    post-critical, 49
    synchronic, 55, 56, 63, 72, 77, 79,
        81, 98
movement of differences, 72
Mukařovský, Jan, 63
mystery, mysteries, 7, 72, 73, 104
    def., 27

narrative, 56, 64, 67, 75–77, 90, 99
    def., 75
narrative criticism, 75–77
natural sciences, 28, 30, 31, 33, 36
    def., 30
negativity
    def., 78

obscurities
    def., 27
ontological vehemence, 18, 20, 38,
    44, 63, 68, 69, 92, 100
ontology, 31, 34, 37, 44, 68, 70, 72,
    100, 104
Origen, 26, 27

parole, 63
participation, 8, 18, 38, 49, 100
paschal mystery, 7, 9, 12, 13, 15, 18,
    19, 43–46, 73, 79, 84
performance, 43, 54, 86
performativity, 85, 86
philology, 24, 87
plot, 65, 75, 76
point of view, 75, 76
polysemy, 40–42
    def., 40
polyvalent, 40, 45, 72
poststructuralism, 70